FOR ORGANS, PIANOS & ELECTRONIC KEYBOARDS

E-Z PLAY® TODAY

235

ELVIS PRESLEY ANTHOLOGY

T0034051

Cover photo Getty Images / Sunset Boulevard / Contributor

ISBN 978-0-7935-2822-6

HAL•LEONARD®

Visit Hal Leonard Online at
www.halleonard.com

Contact us:
Hal Leonard
7777 West Bluemound Road
Milwaukee, WI 53213
Email: info@halleonard.com

In Europe, contact:
Hal Leonard Europe Limited
42 Wigmore Street
Marylebone, London, W1U 2RN
Email: info@halleonardeurope.com

In Australia, contact:
Hal Leonard Australia Pty. Ltd.
4 Lentara Court
Cheltenham, Victoria, 3192 Australia
Email: info@halleonard.com.au

All Shook Up

Registration 4
Rhythm: Rock

Words and Music by Otis Blackwell
and Elvis Presley

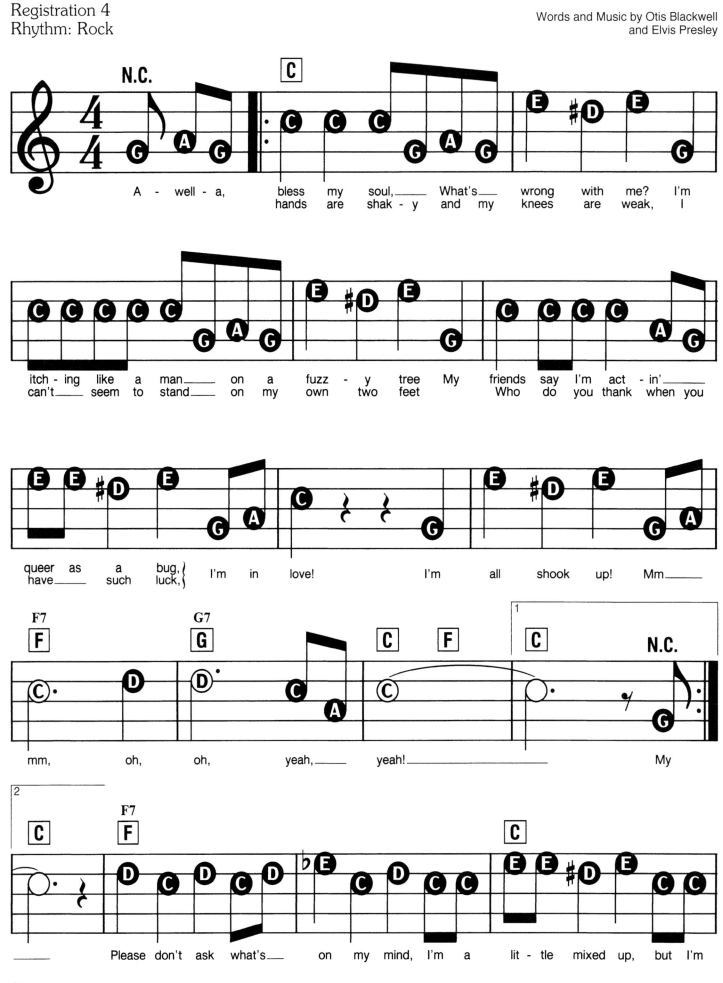

3

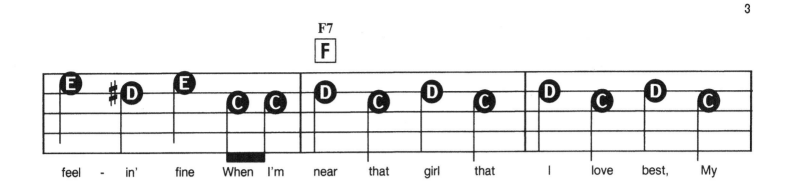

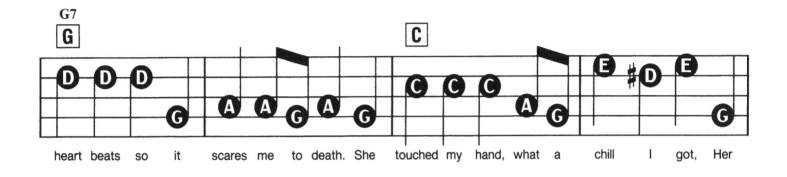

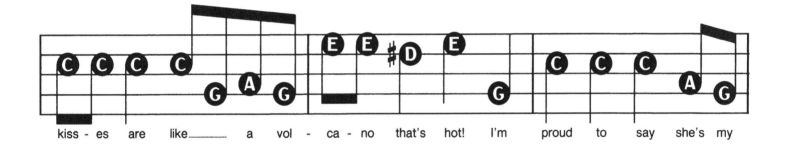

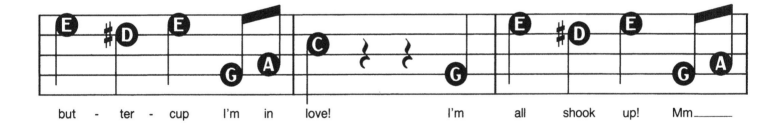

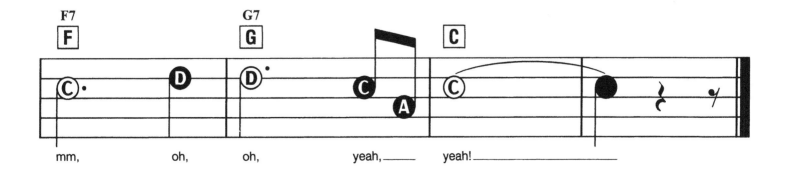

Amazing Grace

Registration 6
Rhythm: Waltz

Words by John Newton
Traditional American Melody
From Carrell and Clayton's *Virginia Harmony*

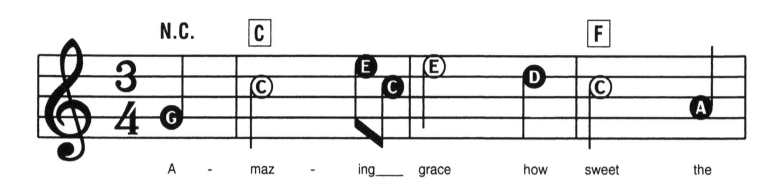

A - maz - ing___ grace how sweet the

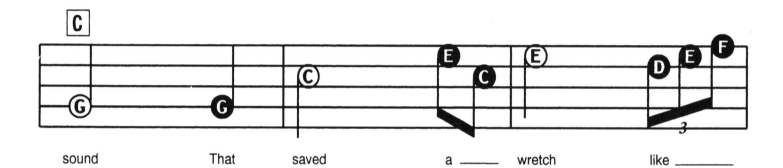

sound   That   saved   a ___ wretch   like _____

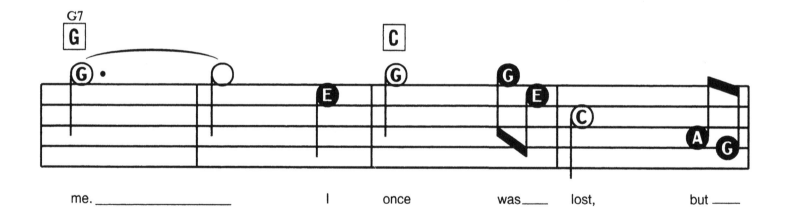

me. _____   I   once   was___ lost,   but ____

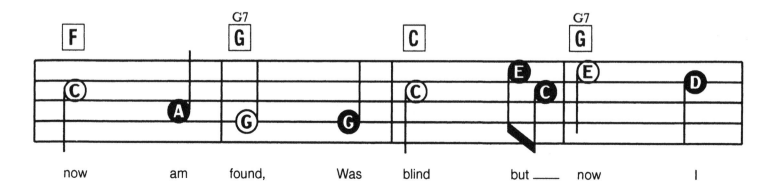

now   am   found,   Was   blind   but ___ now   I

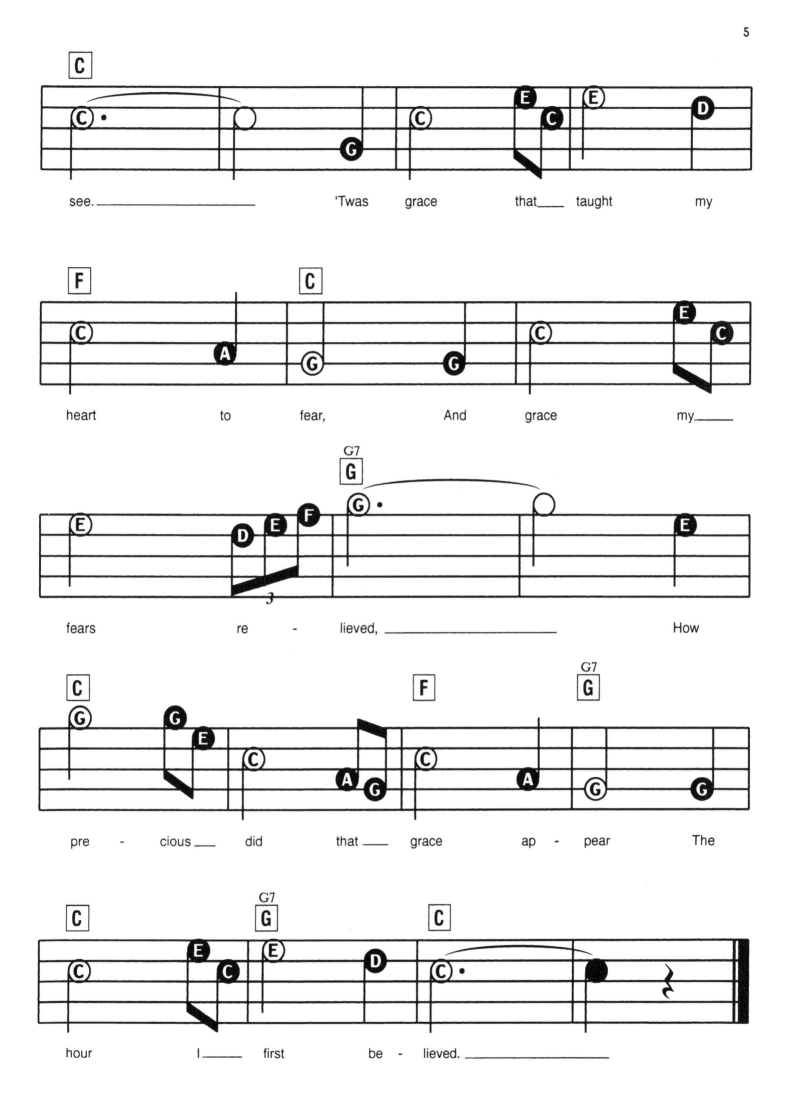

Are You Lonesome Tonight?

Registration 1
Rhythm: Waltz

Words and Music by Roy Turk
and Lou Handman

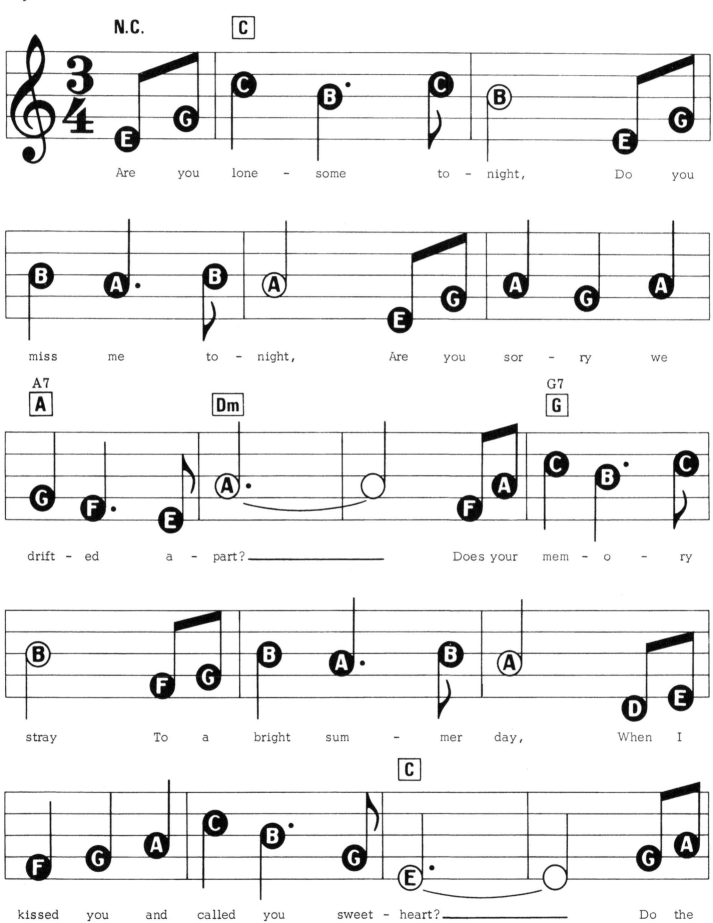

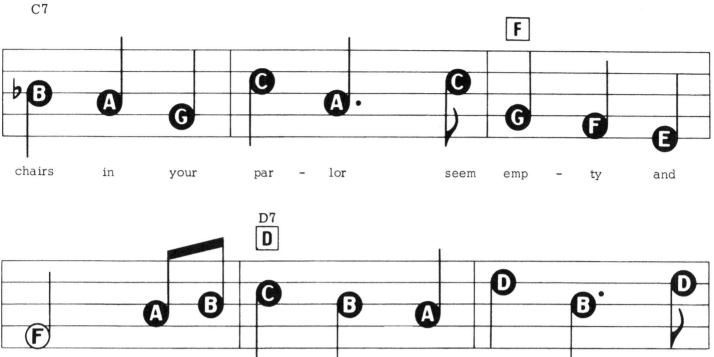

chairs in your par - lor seem emp - ty and

bare? Do you gaze at your door - step and

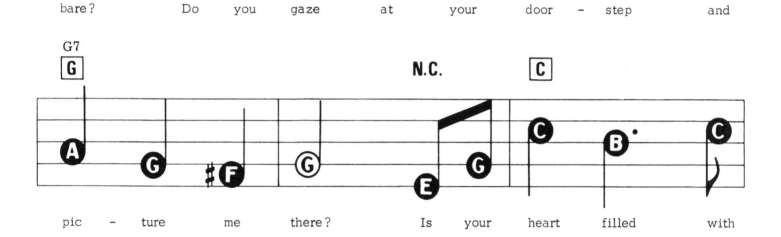

pic - ture me there? Is your heart filled with

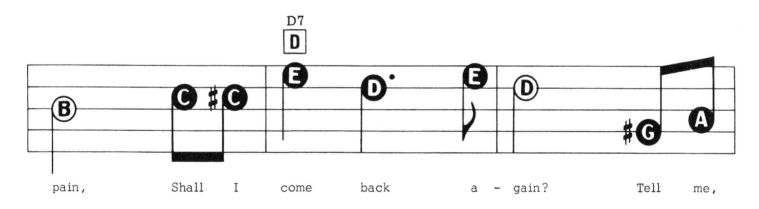

pain, Shall I come back a - gain? Tell me,

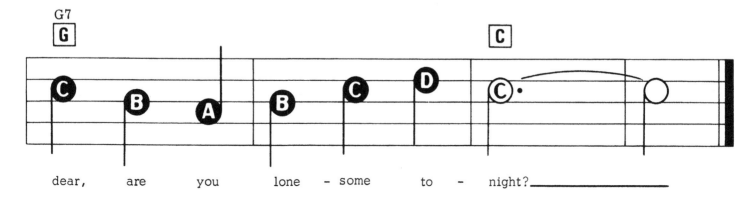

dear, are you lone - some to - night?_____

A Big Hunk o' Love

Registration 5
Rhythm: Rock

Words and Music by Aaron Schroeder
and Sid Wyche

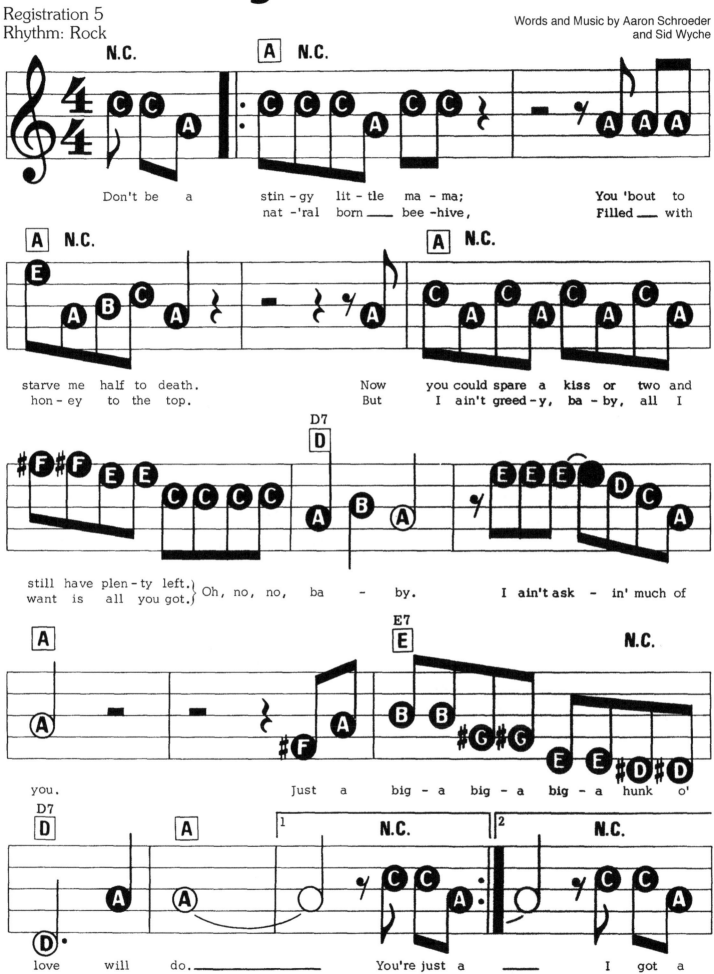

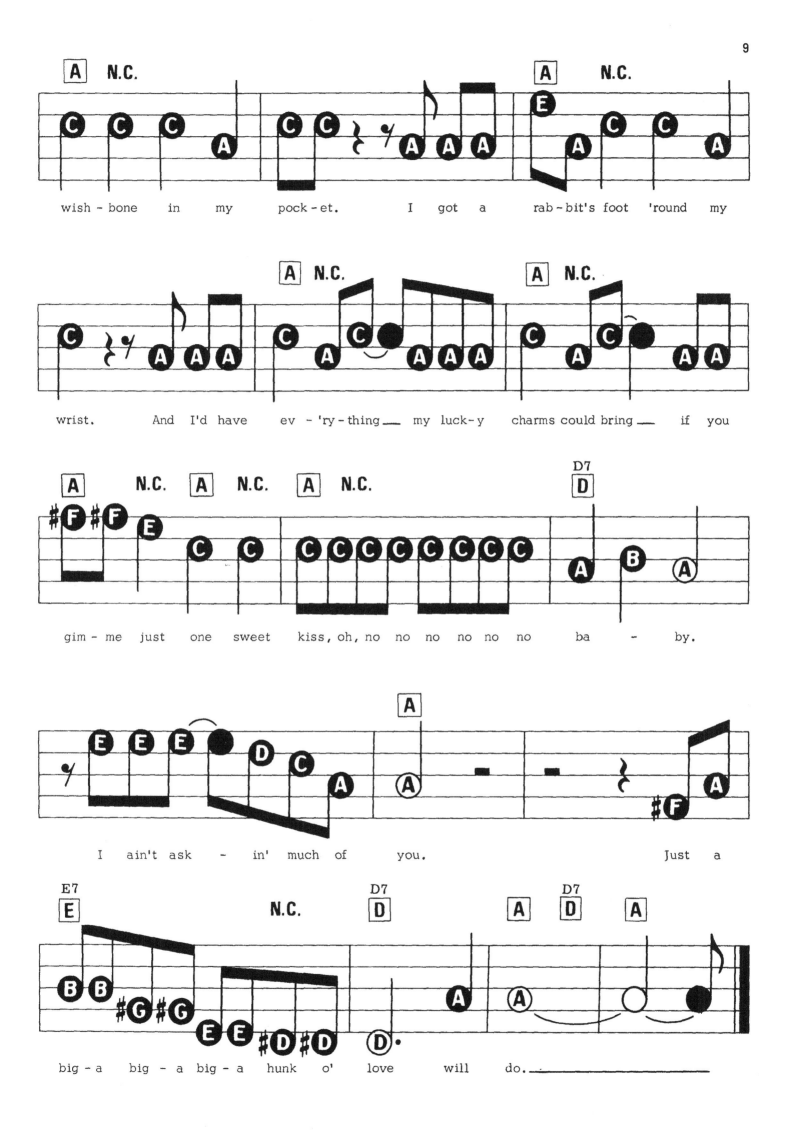

Blue Moon of Kentucky

Registration 1
Rhythm: Swing

Words and Music by
Bill Monroe

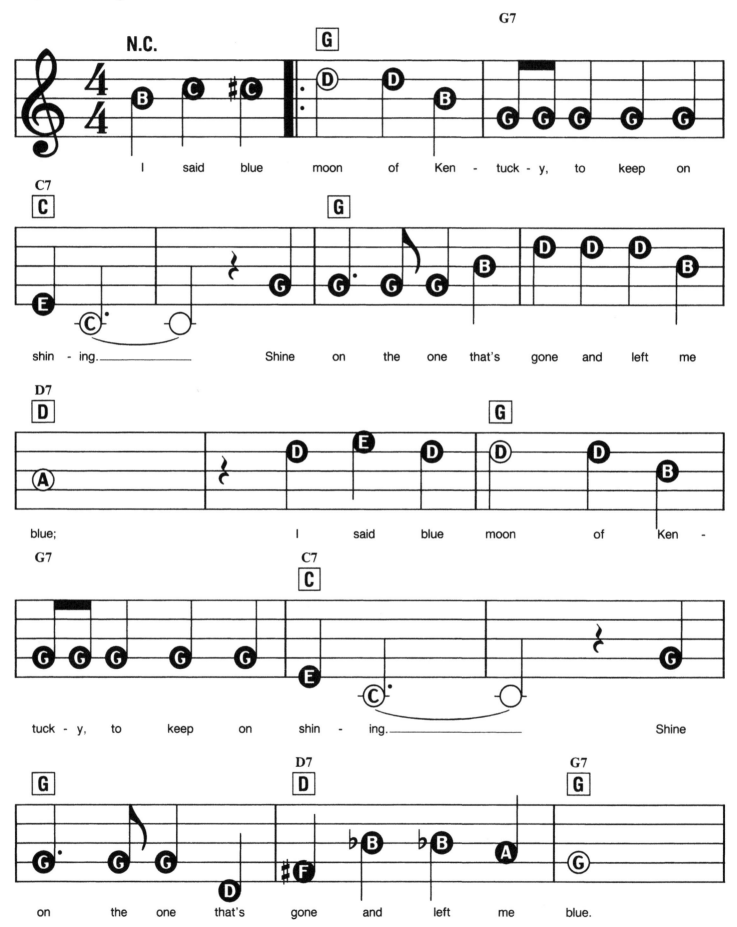

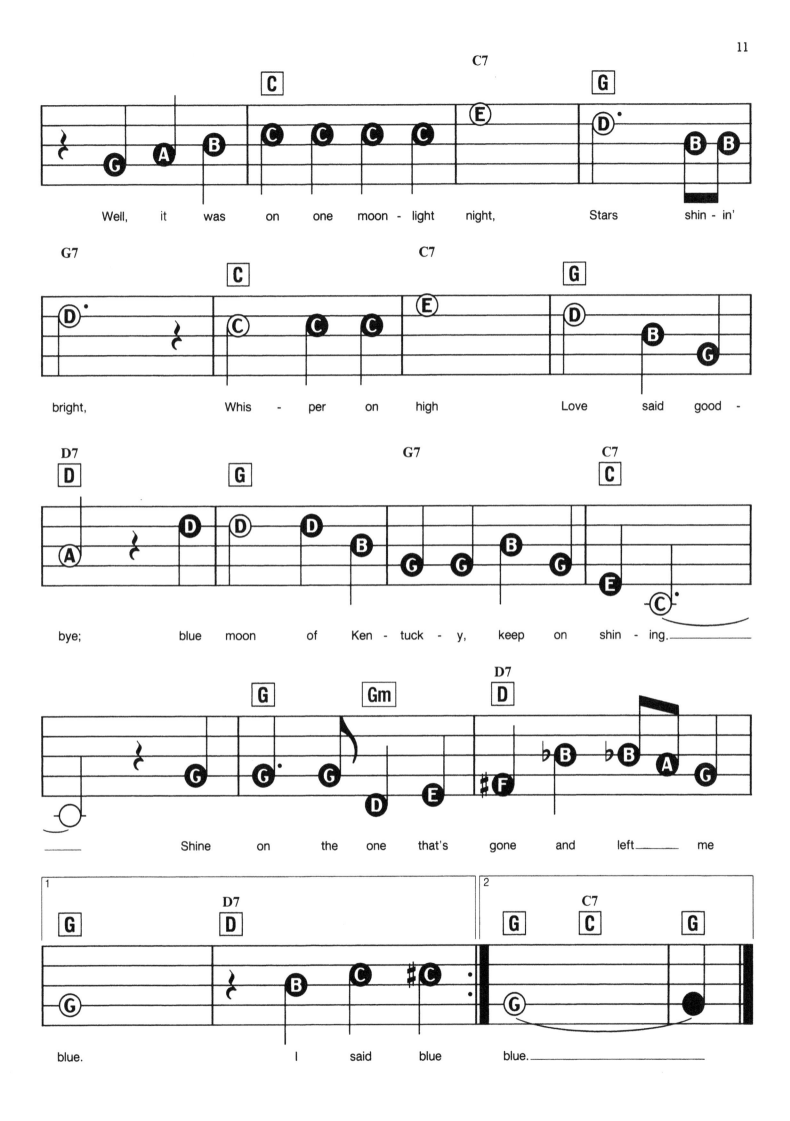

Blue Suede Shoes

Registration 2
Rhythm: Rock

Words and Music by
Carl Lee Perkins

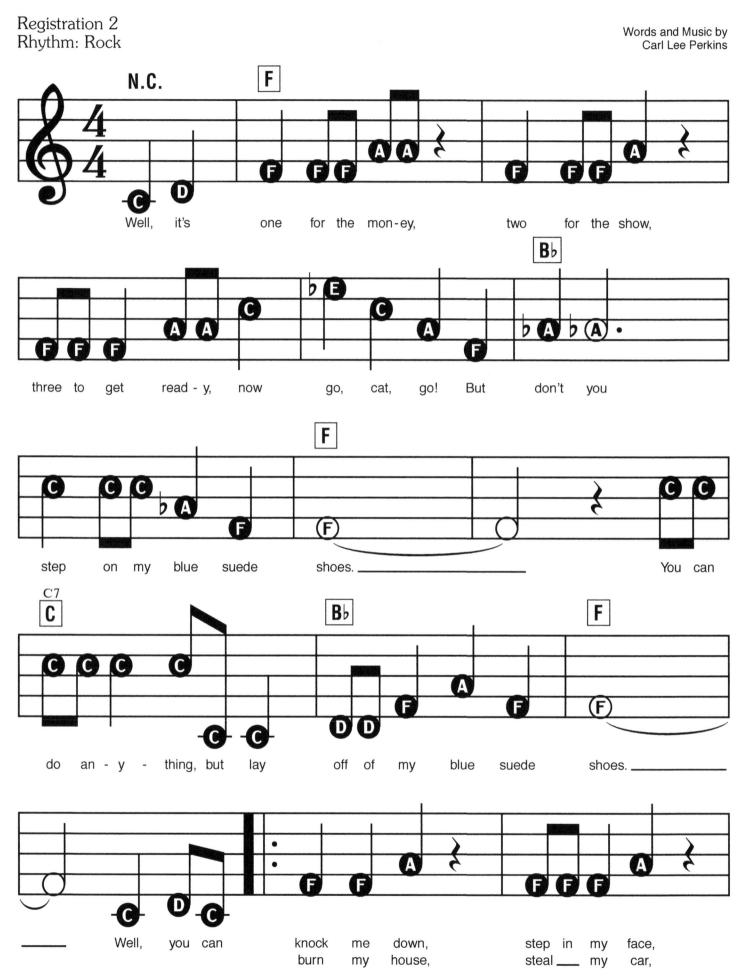

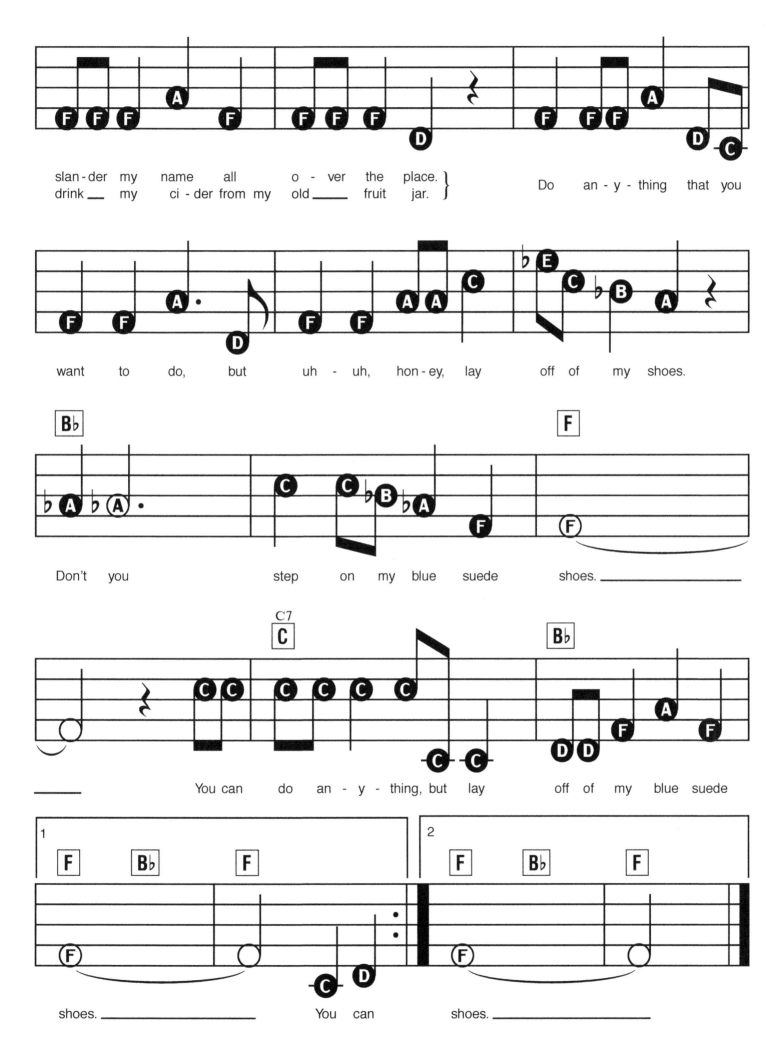

slan-der my name all o - ver the place.
drink __ my ci - der from my old ___ fruit jar.

Do an - y - thing that you

want to do, but uh - uh, hon - ey, lay off of my shoes.

B♭   F

Don't you step on my blue suede shoes. _____

C7
C   B♭

You can do an - y - thing, but lay off of my blue suede

1
F   B♭   F

shoes. _____ You can

2
F   B♭   F

shoes. _____

Burning Love

Registration 1
Rhythm: Rock

Words and Music by
Dennis Linds

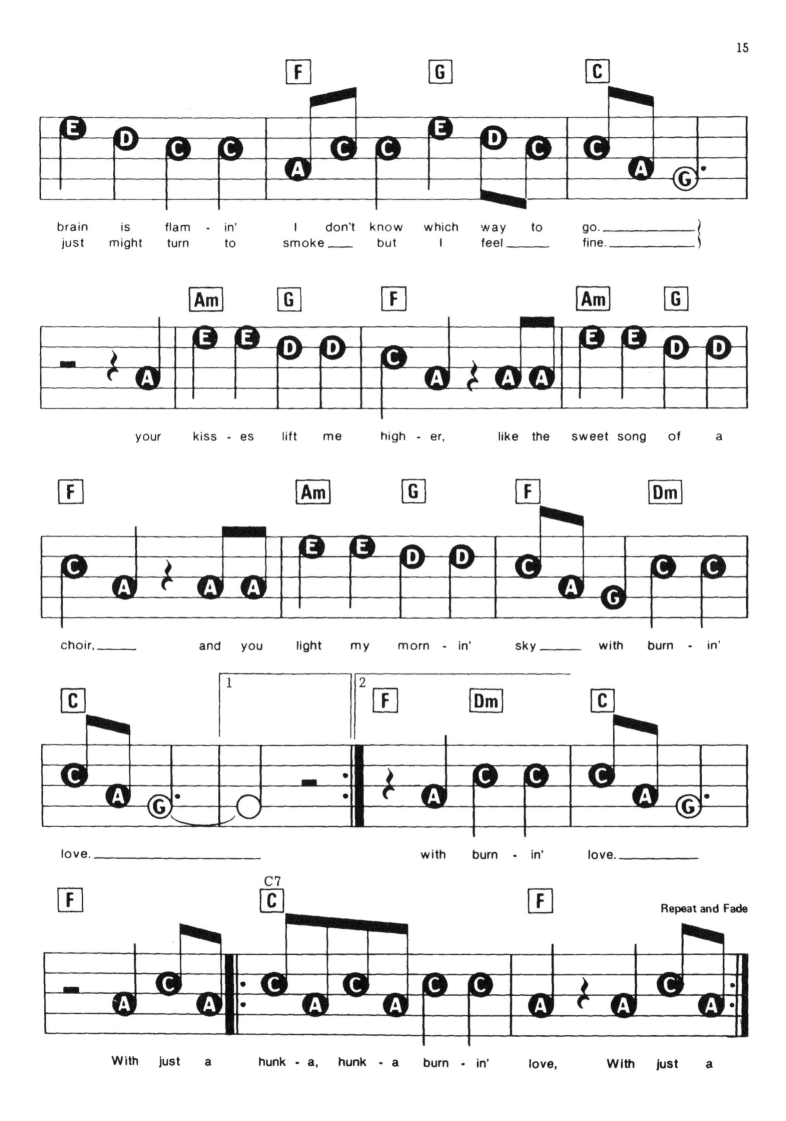

Can't Help Falling in Love
from the Paramount Picture BLUE HAWAII

Registration 3
Rhythm: Ballad or Swing

Words and Music by George David Weiss,
Hugo Peretti and Luigi Creatore

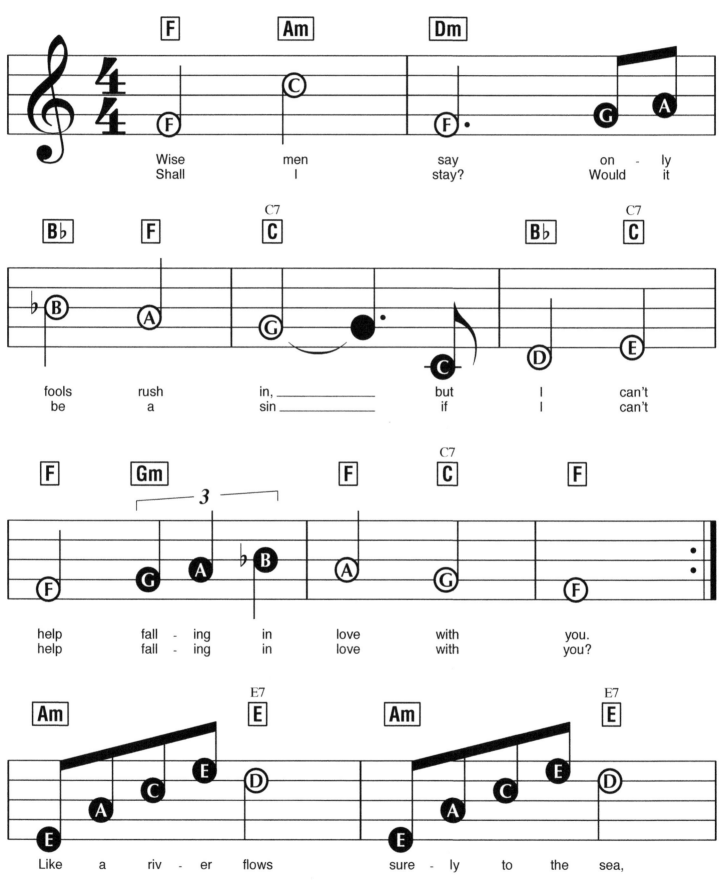

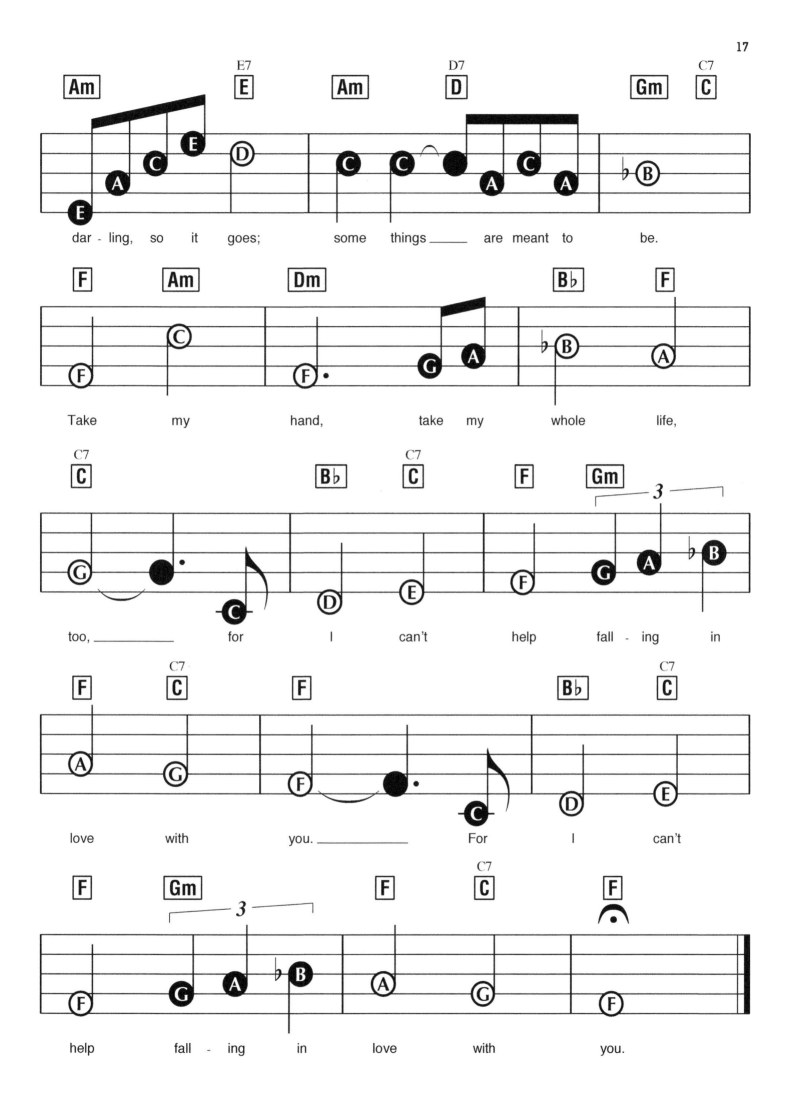

17

Cryin' in the Chapel

Registration 2
Rhythm: Ballad or Fox Trot

Written by
Artie Glenn

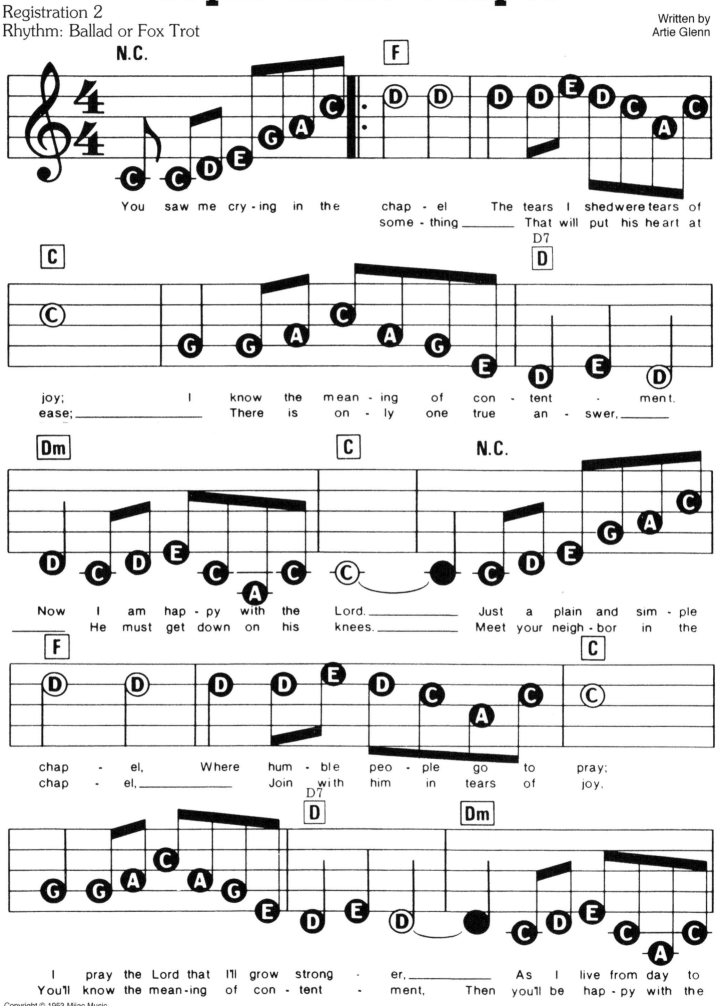

Don't

Registration 1
Rhythm: Slow Rock or Fifties Ballad

Words and Music by Jerry Leiber
and Mike Stoller

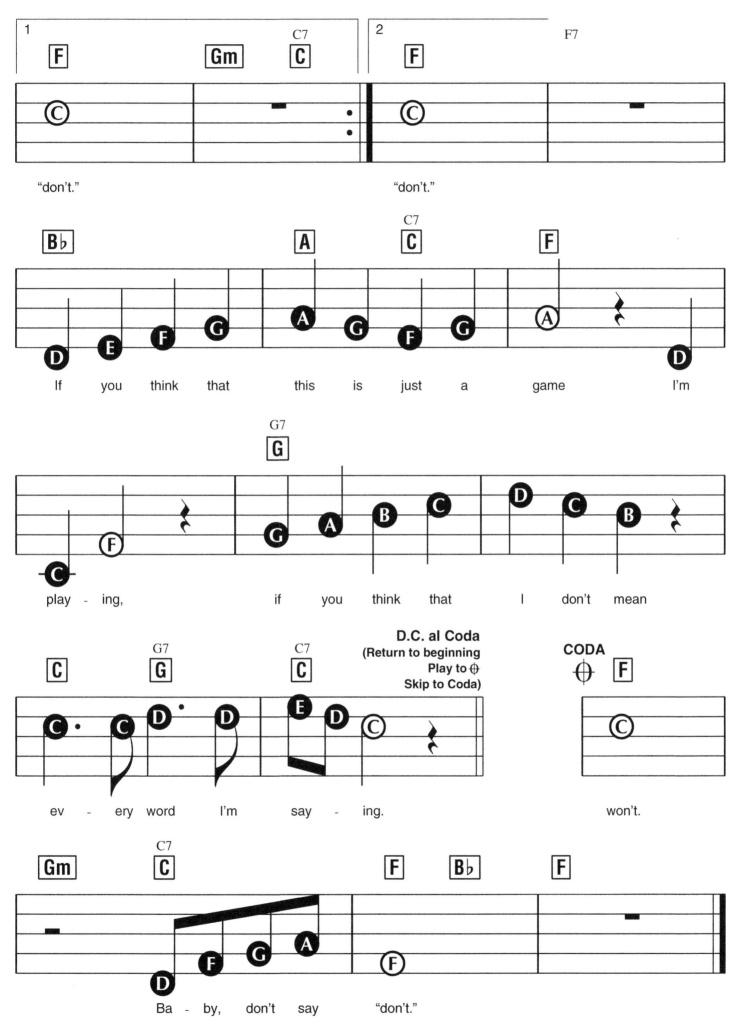

Don't Be Cruel
(To a Heart That's True)

Registration 10
Rhythm: Rock

Words and Music by Otis Blackwell
and Elvis Presley

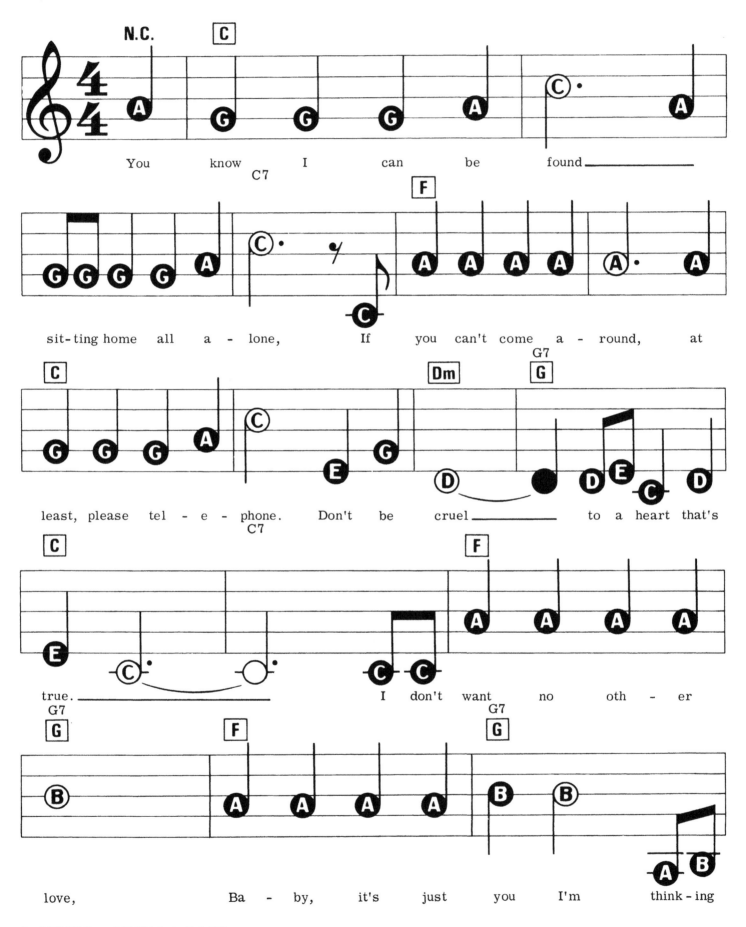

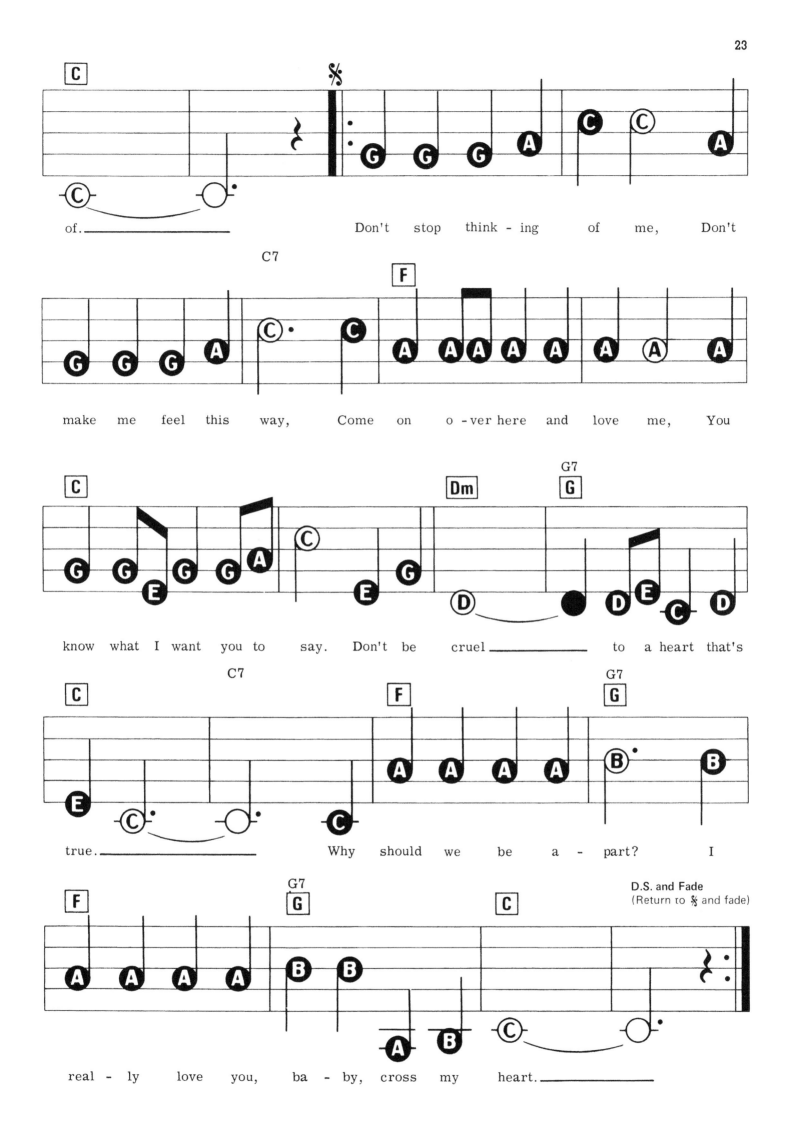

Don't Cry Daddy

Registration 4
Rhythm: Rock

Words and Music by
Scott Davis

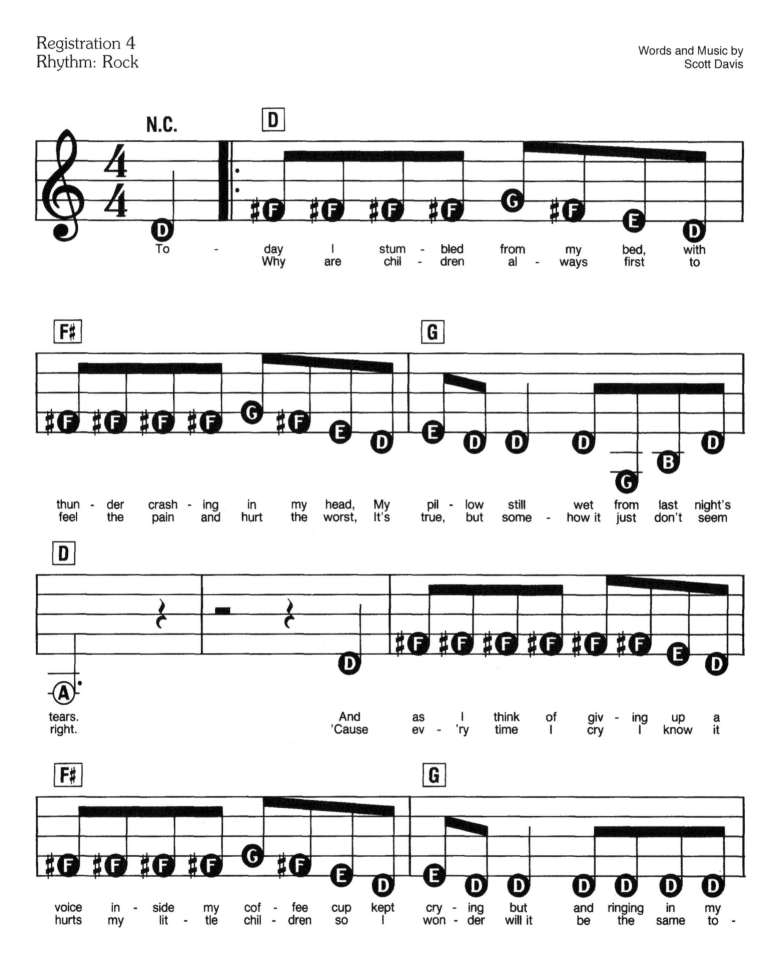

25

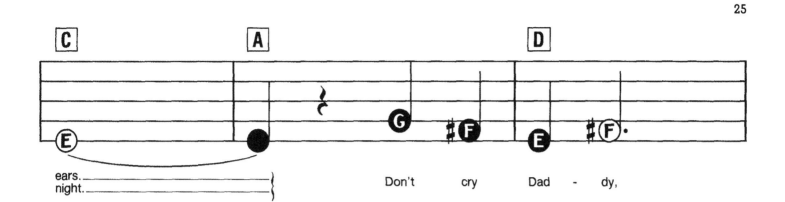

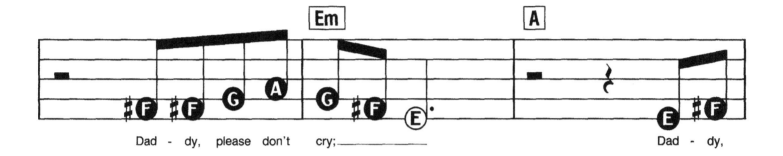

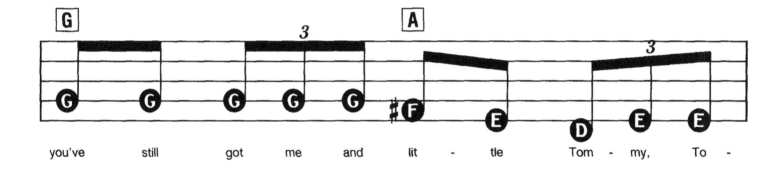

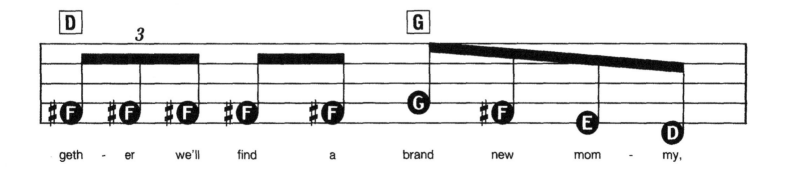

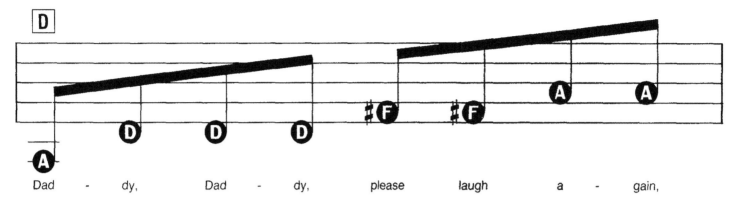

Dad - dy, Dad - dy, please laugh a - gain,

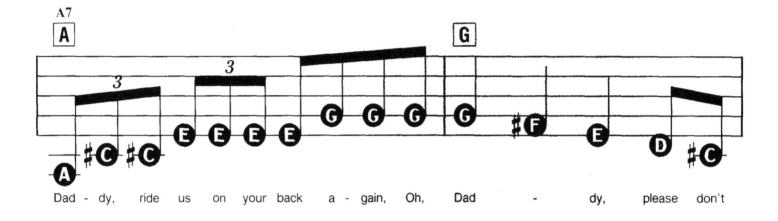

Dad - dy, ride us on your back a - gain, Oh, Dad - dy, please don't

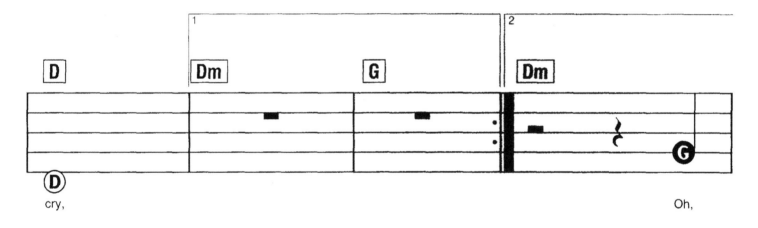

cry, Oh,

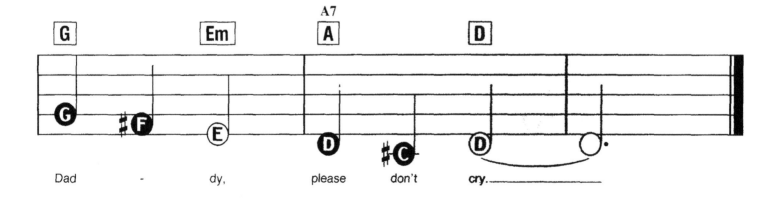

Dad - dy, please don't cry.

Hard Headed Woman

Registration 8
Rhythm: Rock

Words and Music by
Claude De Metruis

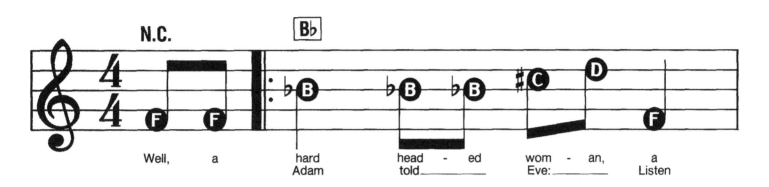

Well, a   hard   head - ed   wom - an,   a
Adam   told ____   Eve: ___   Listen

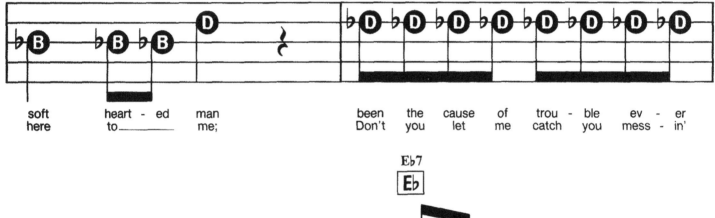

soft   heart - ed   man   been   the   cause   of   trou - ble   ev - er
here   to _____   me;   Don't   you   let   me   catch   you   mess - in'

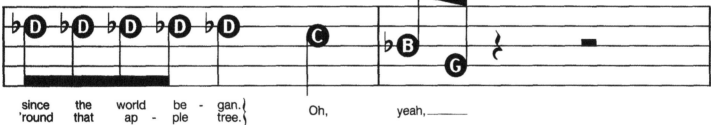

since   the   world   be - gan.   Oh,   yeah, _____
'round   that   world   ap - ple   tree.

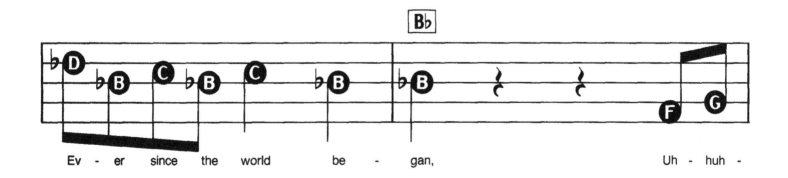

Ev - er   since   the   world   be - gan,   Uh - huh -

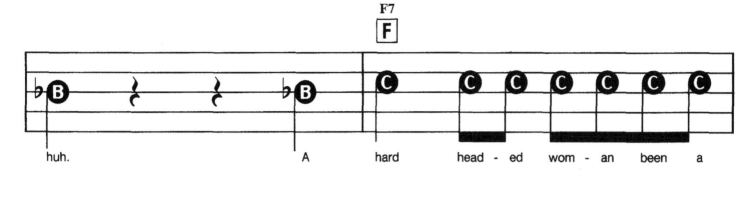

huh.   A   hard   head - ed   wom - an   been   a

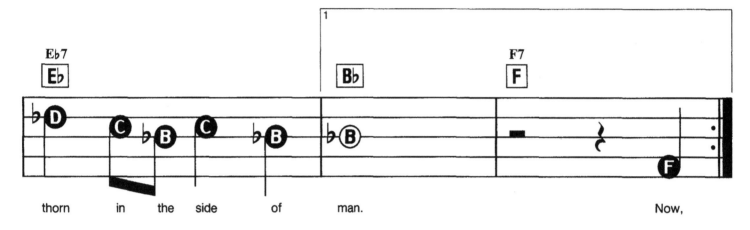

thorn   in   the   side   of   man.   Now,

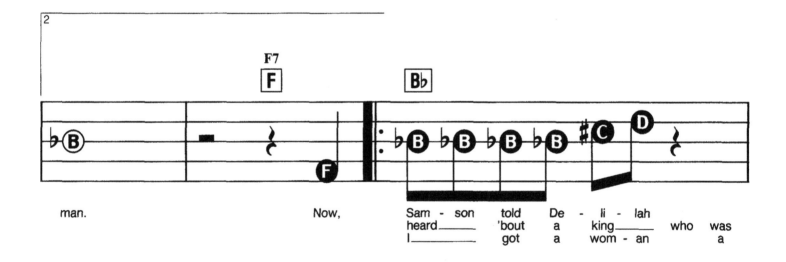

man.   Now,

Sam - son   told   De - li - lah   who   was
heard_____   'bout   a   king_____   who   was
I_____   got   a   wom - an   a

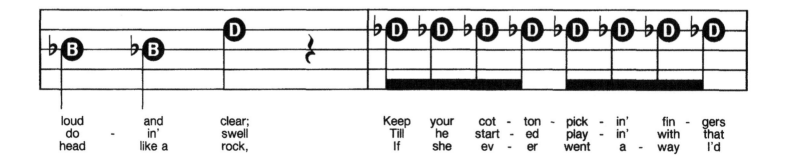

loud   and   clear;   Keep   your   cot - ton - pick - in'   fin - gers
do -   in'   swell   Till   he   start - ed   play - in'   with   that
head   like a   rock,   If   she   ev - er   went   a - way   I'd

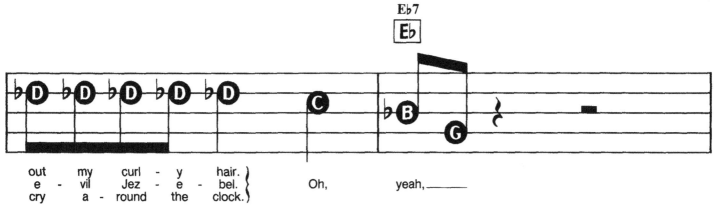

out   my   curl - y   hair. ⎫
e - vil   Jez - e - bel. ⎬
cry   a - round   the   clock. ⎭

Oh,   yeah,_____

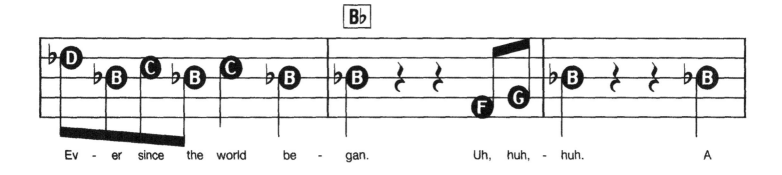

Ev - er   since   the   world   be - gan.   Uh,   huh, - huh.   A

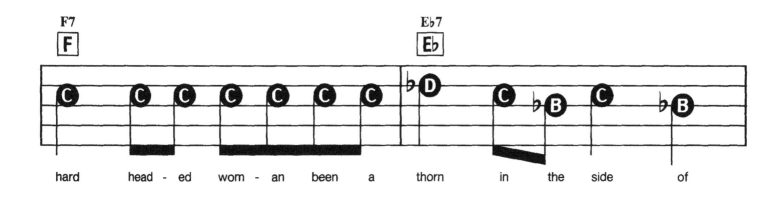

hard   head - ed   wom - an   been   a   thorn   in   the   side   of

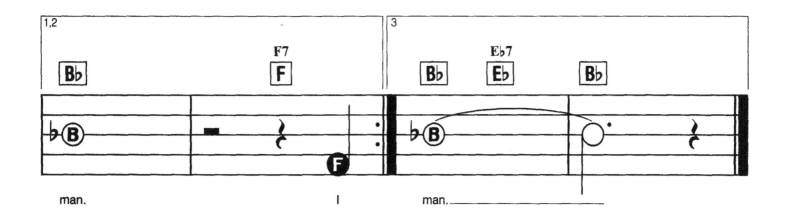

man.   I   man._____

(Now and Then There's)
A Fool Such As I

Registration 7
Rhythm: Swing

Words and Music by
Bill Trader

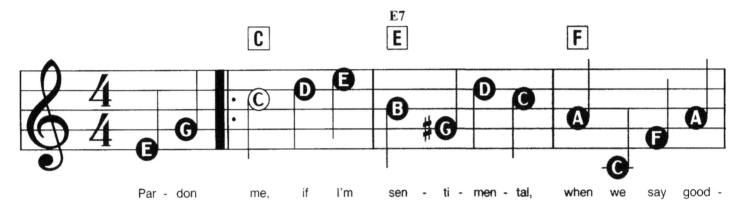

Par - don me, if I'm sen - ti - men - tal, when we say good -

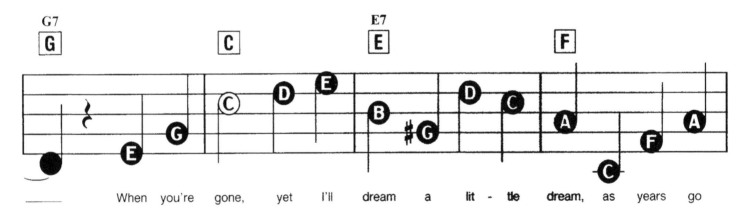

bye, Don't be an - gry with me, should I cry._

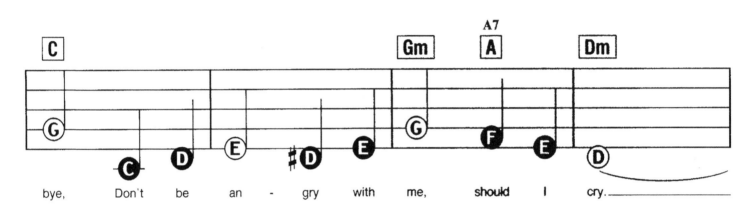

When you're gone, yet I'll dream a lit - tle dream, as years go

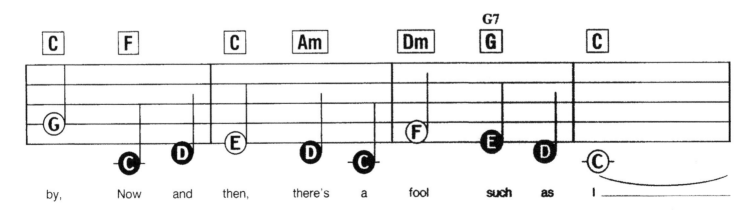

by, Now and then, there's a fool such as I_

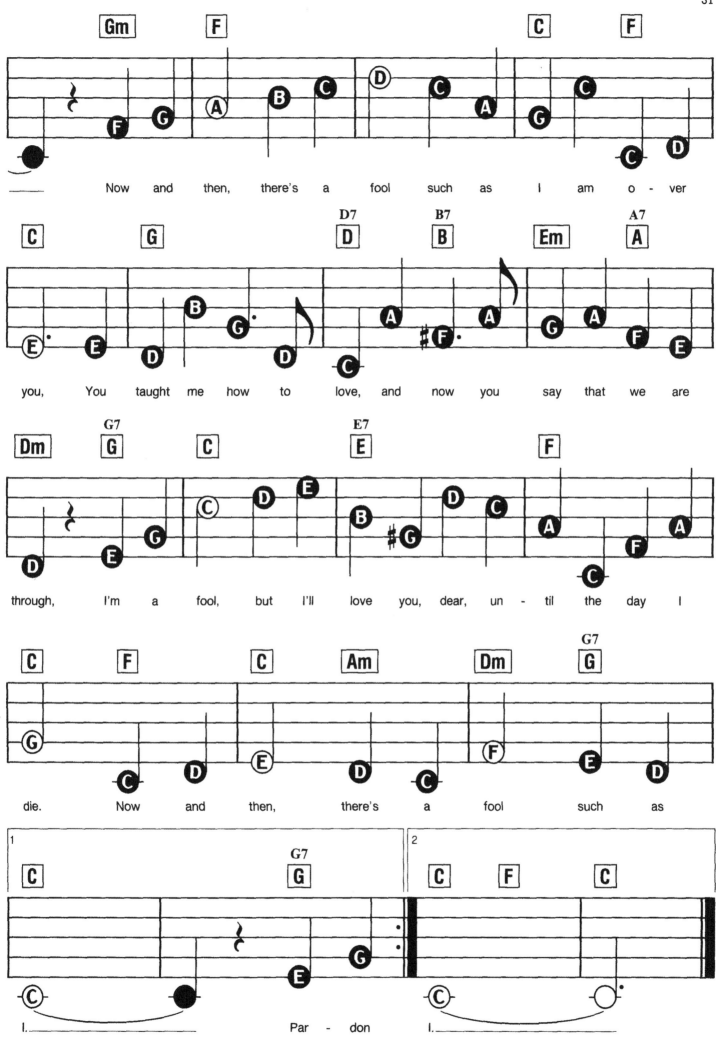

G.I. Blues

Registration 2
Rhythm: Rock

Words and Music by Sid Tepper
and Roy C. Bennett

They

give us a room with a view of the beau - ti - ful
get has - sen - fef - fer and black pump - er - nick - el for
Frau - leins are pret - ty as flow'rs, but we can't make a

Rhine.
chow.
march.
pass.

They give us a room with a
We get has - sen - fef - fer and
We'd like to be he - roes, but
The Frau - leins are pret - ty as

view of the beau - ti - ful Rhine.
black pump - er - nick - el for chow.
all that we do here is march.
flow'rs, but we can't make a pass.

Gim - me a
I'd blow my
And they
'Cause they're

mud - dy old creek in Tex - as an - y old time.
next___ month's pay for a slice of Tex - as cow.
don't___ give the Pur - ple Heart for a fall - en arch.
all___ wearin' signs sayin', "Keepen Sie off___ the grass!"

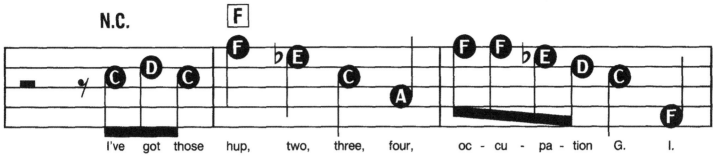

I've got those hup, two, three, four, oc - cu - pa - tion G. I.

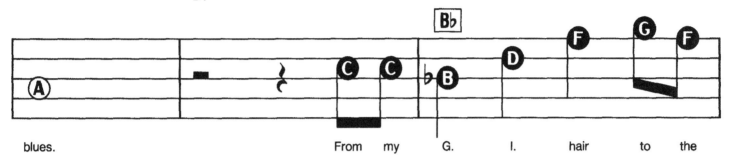

blues. From my G. I. hair to the

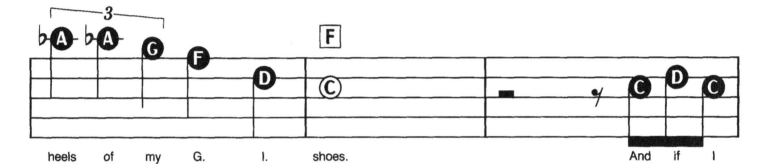

heels of my G. I. shoes. And if I

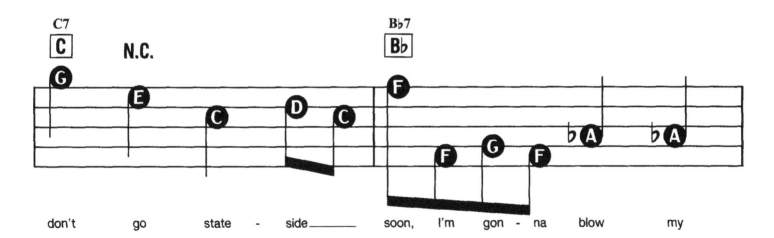

don't go state - side soon, I'm gon - na blow my

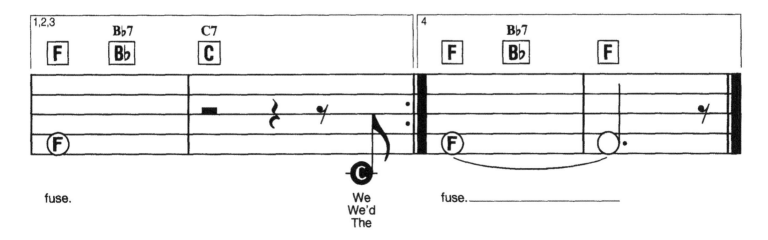

fuse.   We   fuse.
         We'd
         The

Good Luck Charm

Registration 4
Rhythm: Rock

Words and Music by Aaron Schroeder
and Wally Gold

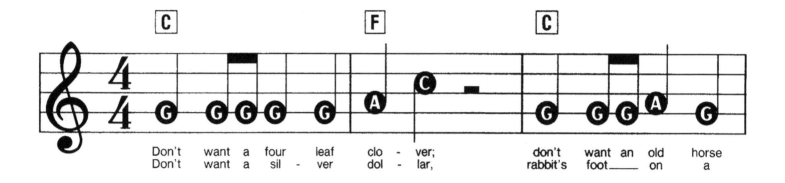

Don't want a four leaf clo - ver;   don't want an old horse
Don't want a sil - ver dol - lar,   rabbit's foot____ on a

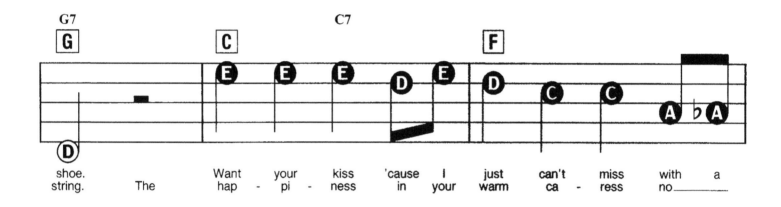

shoe.   The   Want your kiss 'cause I just can't miss with a
string.   The   hap - pi - ness in your warm ca - ress no____

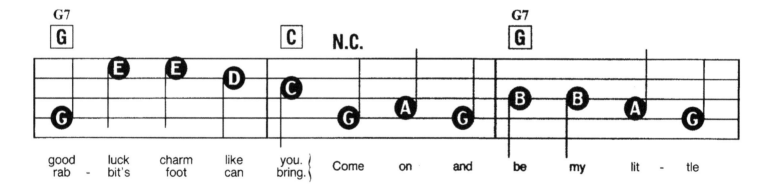

good luck charm like you.   Come on and be my lit - tle
rab - bit's foot can bring.

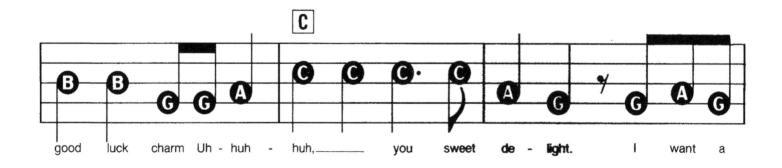

good luck charm Uh - huh - huh,____ you sweet de - light.   I want a

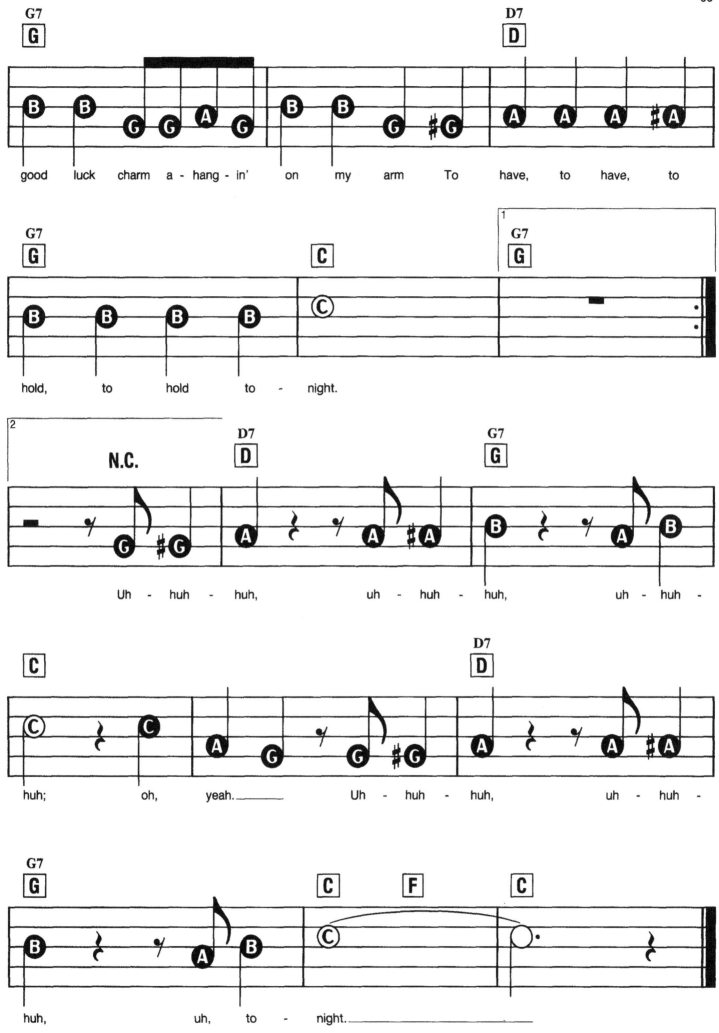

The Hawaiian Wedding Song
(Ke Kali Nei Au)

Registration 1
Rhythm: Ballad or Fox Trot

English Lyrics by Al Hoffman and Dick Manning
Hawaiian Lyrics and Music by Charles E. King

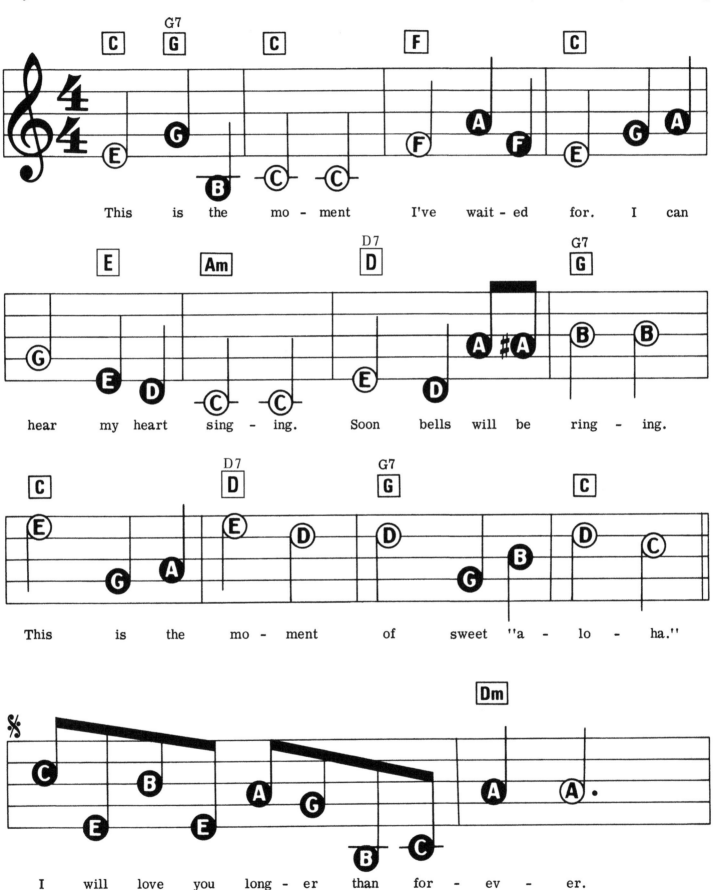

This is the mo - ment I've wait - ed for. I can

hear my heart sing - ing. Soon bells will be ring - ing.

This is the mo - ment of sweet "a - lo - ha."

I will love you long - er than for - ev - er.
Prom - ise me that you will leave me ne - ver.

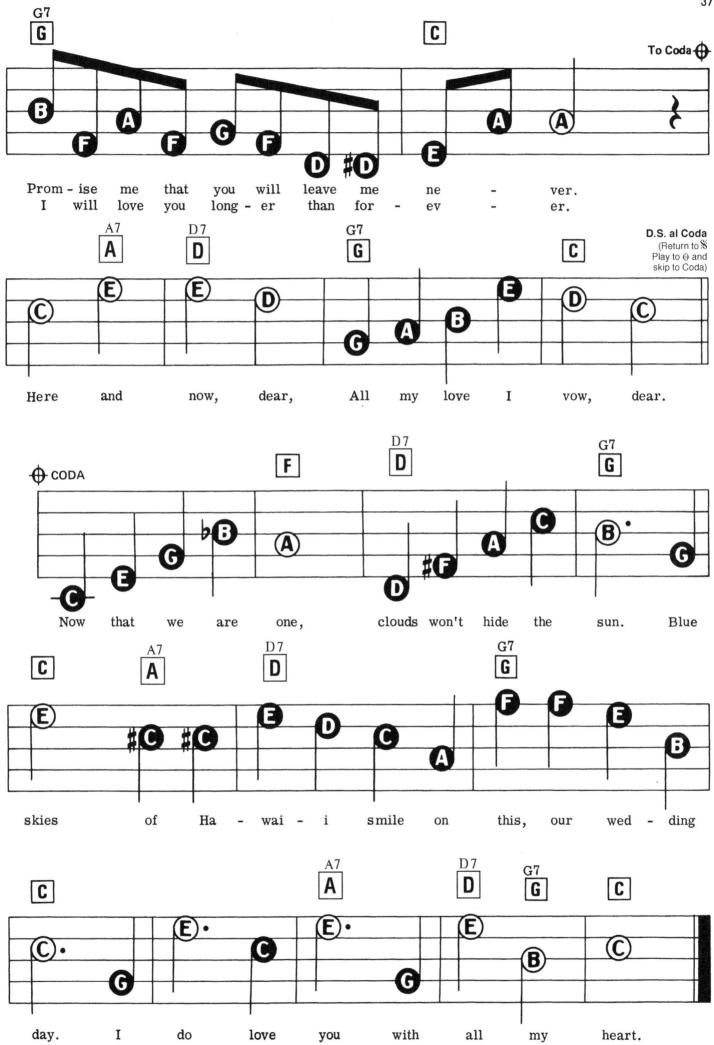

Heartbreak Hotel

Registration 4
Rhythm: Rock

Words and Music by Mae Boren Axton,
Tommy Durden and Elvis Presley

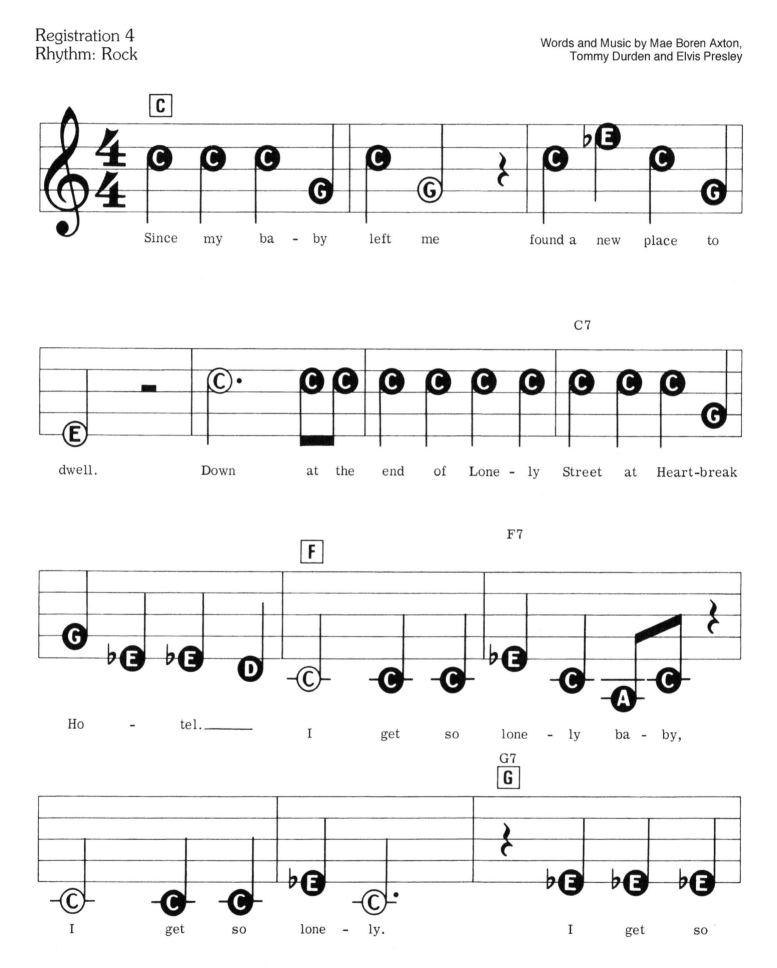

39

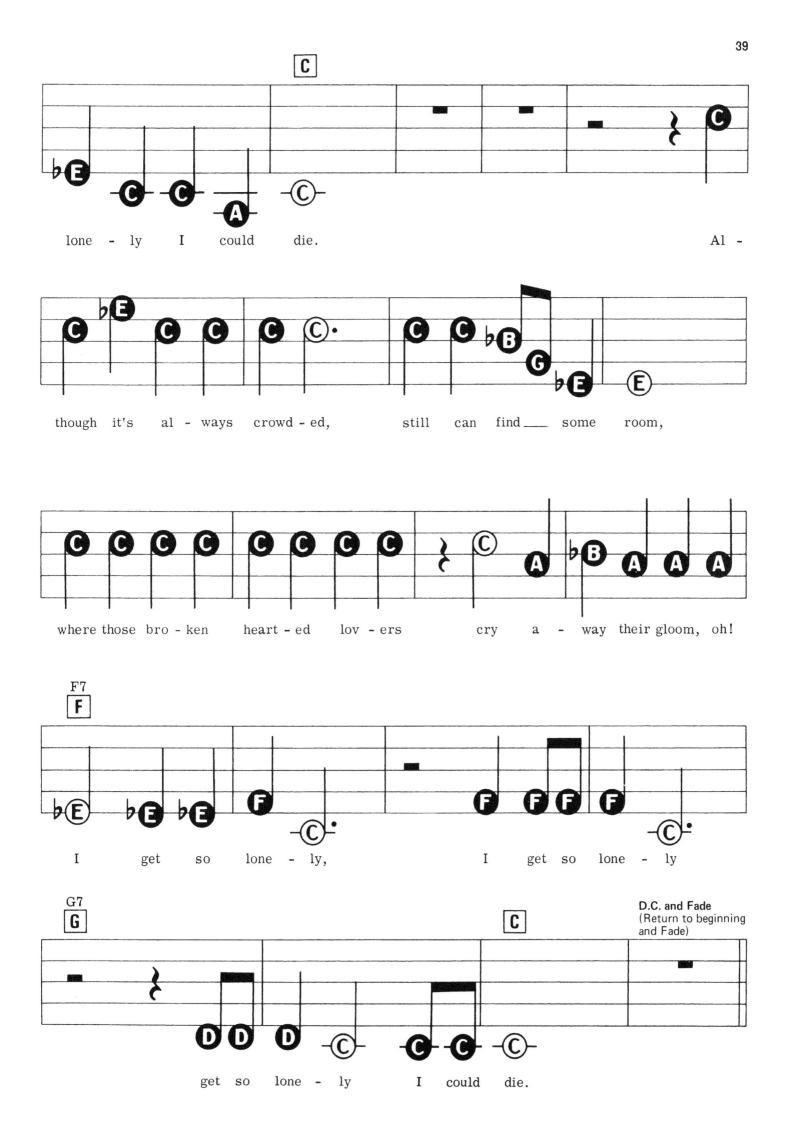

Hound Dog

Registration 7
Rhythm: Rock

Words and Music by Jerry Leiber
and Mike Stoller

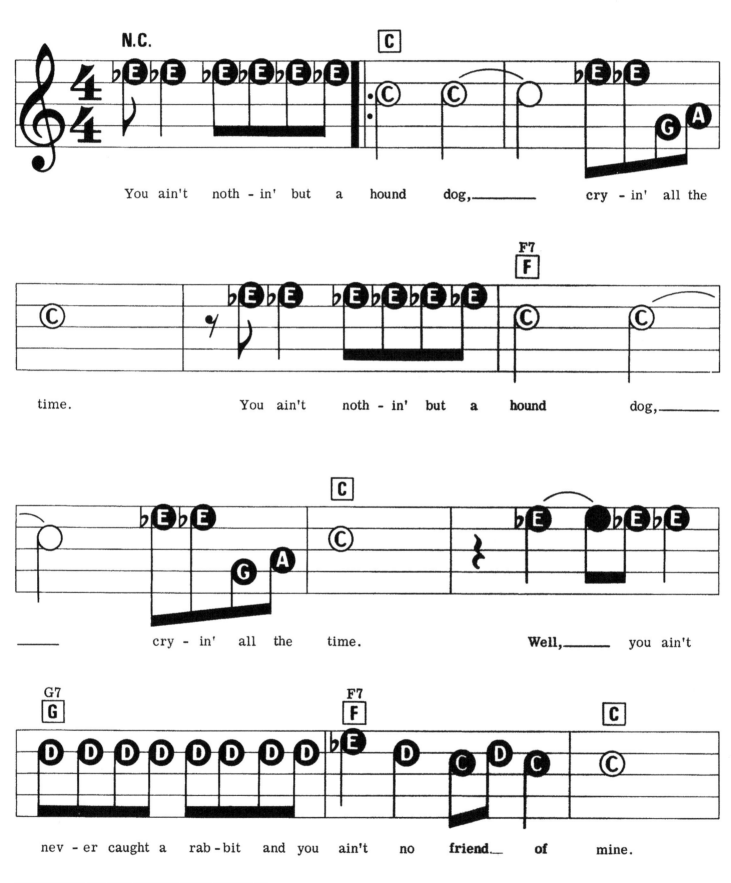

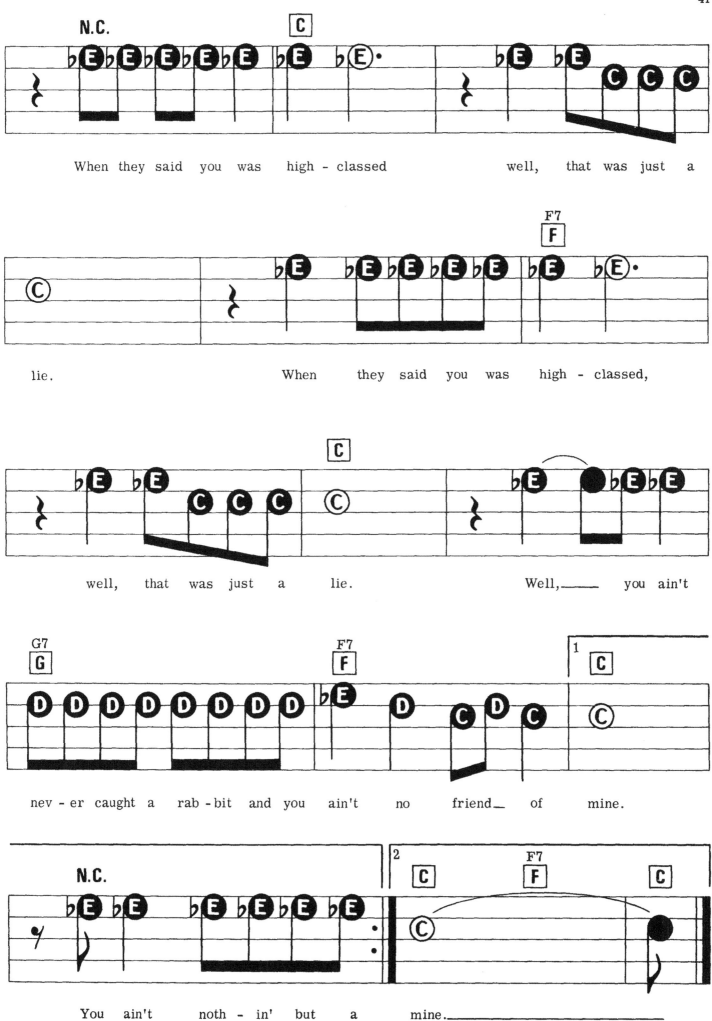

When they said you was high - classed well, that was just a

lie. When they said you was high - classed,

well, that was just a lie. Well,____ you ain't

nev - er caught a rab - bit and you ain't no friend__ of mine.

You ain't noth - in' but a mine._____

I Beg of You

Registration 2
Rhythm: Rock

Words and Music by Rose Marie McCoy
and Kelly Owens

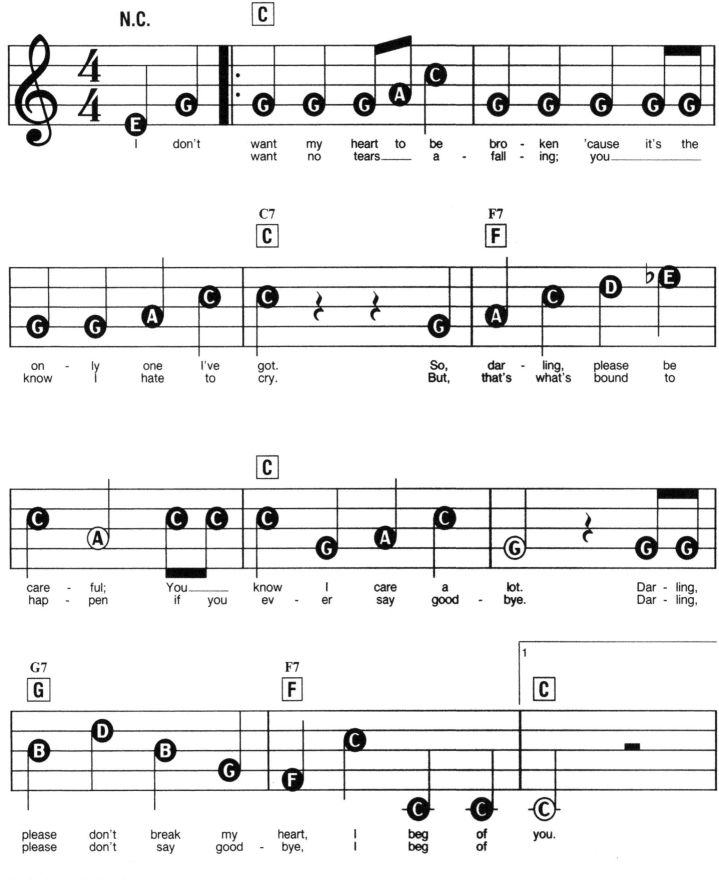

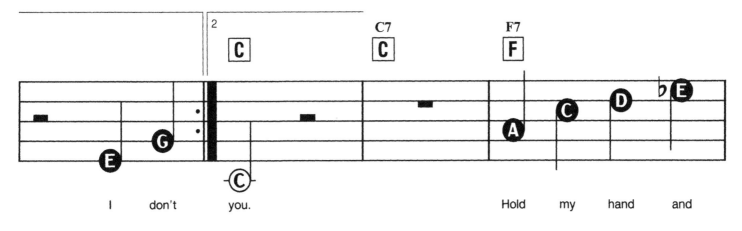

I don't you. Hold my hand and

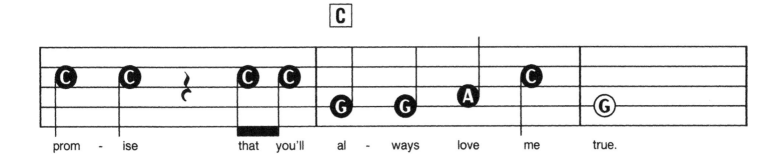

prom - ise that you'll al - ways love me true.

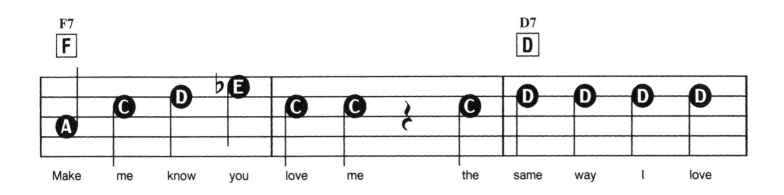

Make me know you love me the same way I love

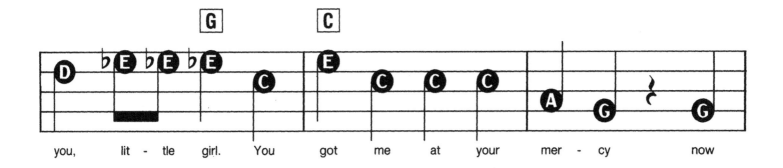

you, lit - tle girl. You got me at your mer - cy now

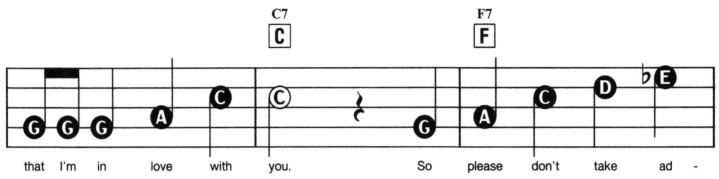

that I'm in love with you. So please don't take ad -

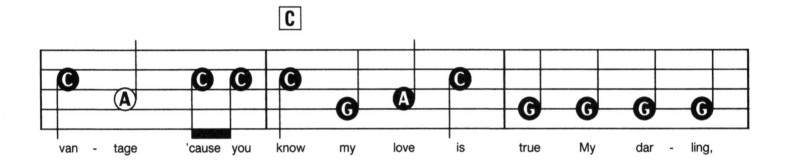

van - tage 'cause you know my love is true My dar - ling,

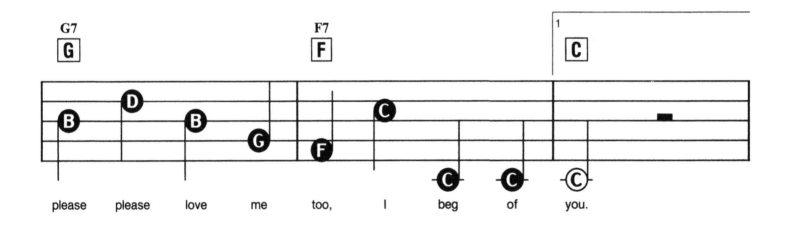

please please love me too, I beg of you.

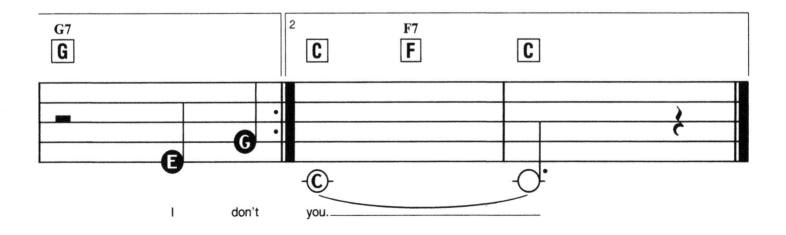

I don't you._____

I Believe

Registration 2
Rhythm: Ballad or Slow Rock

Words and Music by Ervin Drake,
Irvin Graham, Jimmy Shirl and Al Stillman

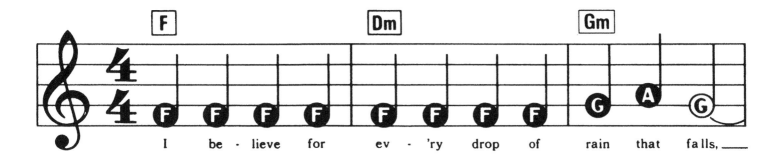

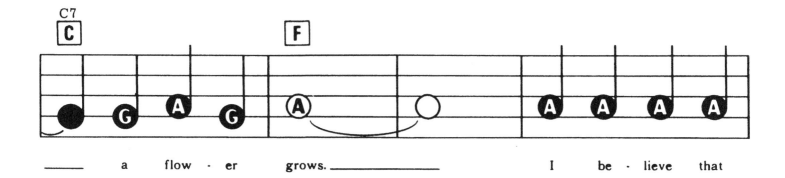

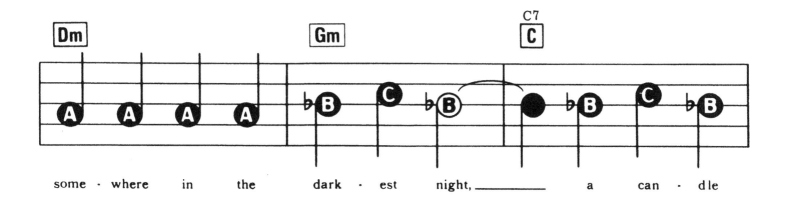

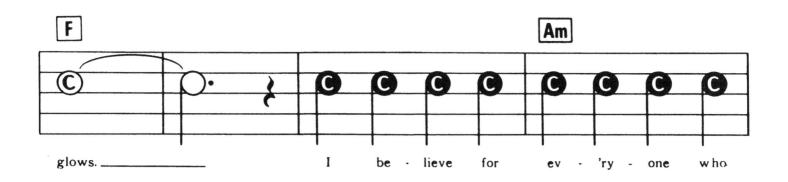

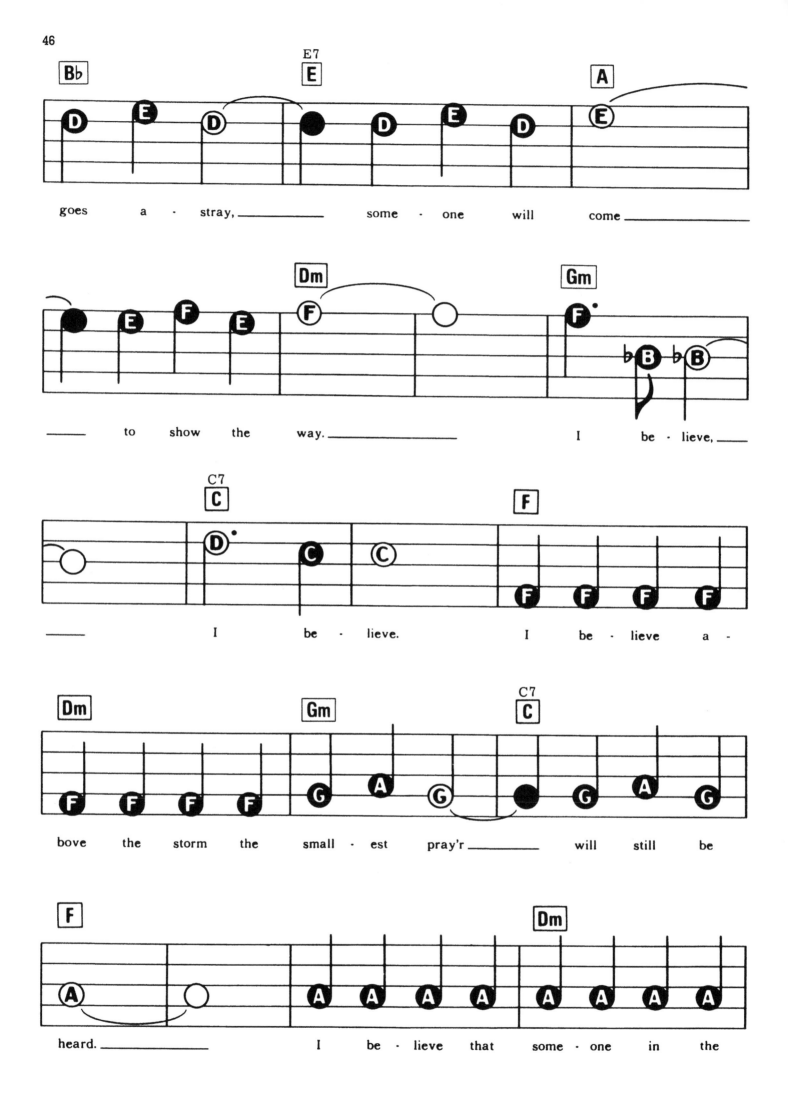

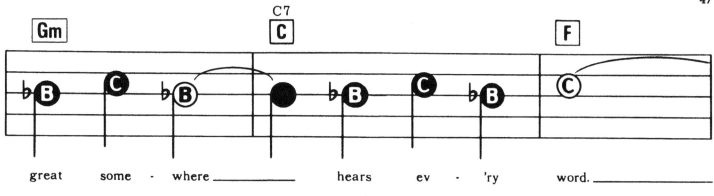

great some - where _____ hears ev - 'ry word. _____

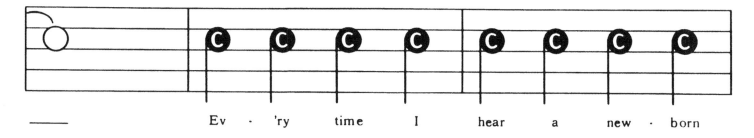

_____ Ev - 'ry time I hear a new - born

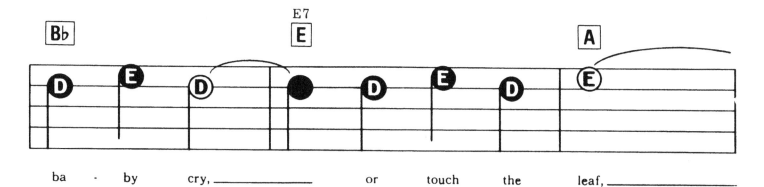

ba - by cry, _____ or touch the leaf, _____

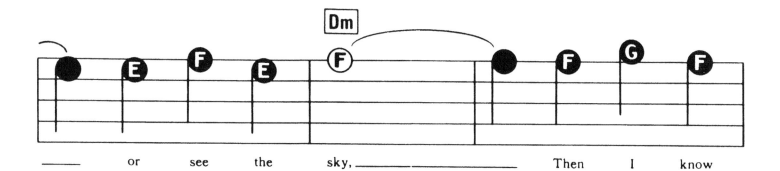

_____ or see the sky, _____ Then I know

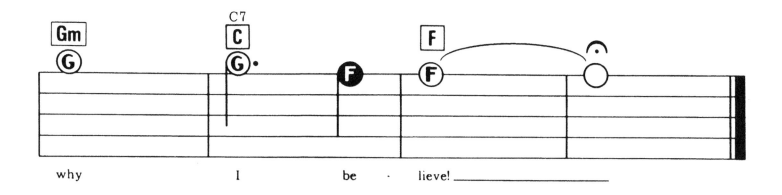

why I be - lieve! _____

I Got a Woman

Registration 4
Rhythm: Rock

Words and Music by Ray Charles
and Renald J. Richard

I Got Stung

Registration 4
Rhythm: Rock

Words and Music by Aaron Schroeder
and David Hill

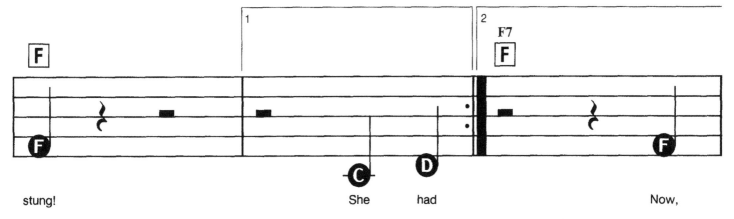

stung! She had Now,

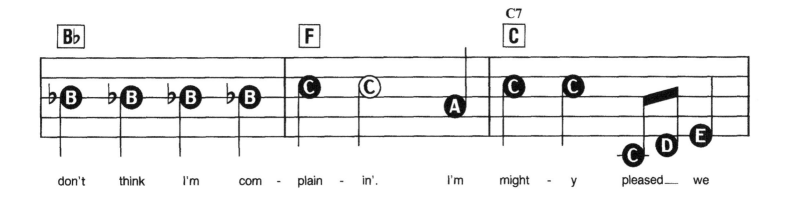

don't think I'm com - plain - in'. I'm might - y pleased___ we

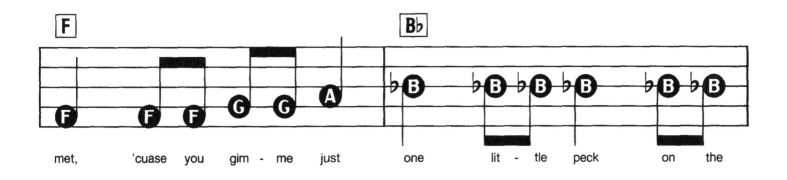

met, 'cuase you gim - me just one lit - tle peck on the

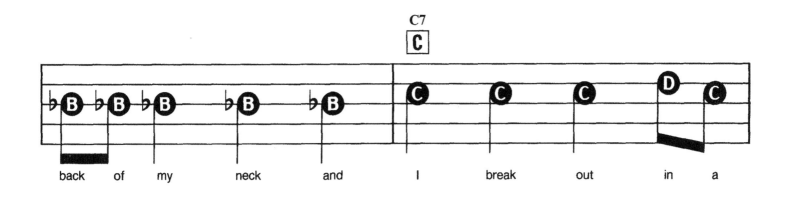

back of my neck and I break out in a

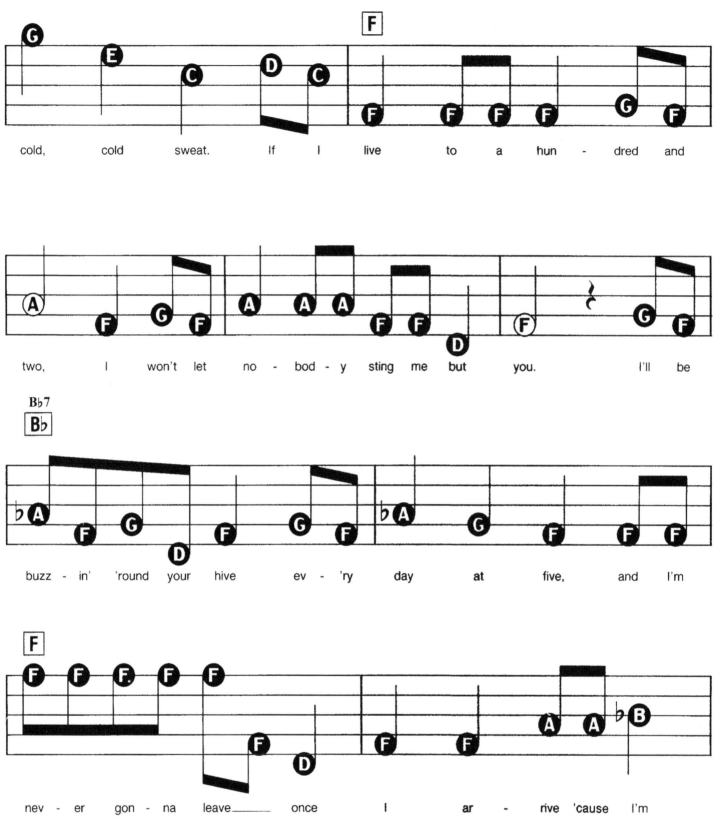

cold,   cold   sweat.   If   I   live   to   a   hun - dred   and

two,   I   won't   let   no - bod - y   sting   me   but   you.   I'll   be

buzz - in'   'round   your   hive   ev - 'ry   day   at   five,   and   I'm

nev - er   gon - na   leave_____   once   I   ar - rive   'cause   I'm

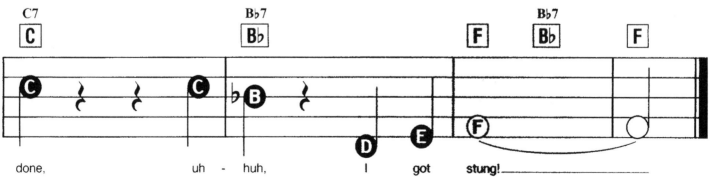

done,   uh - huh,   I   got   stung!_____

In the Ghetto
(The Vicious Circle)

Registration 4
Rhythm: Ballad or Slow Rock

Words and Music by
Mac Davis

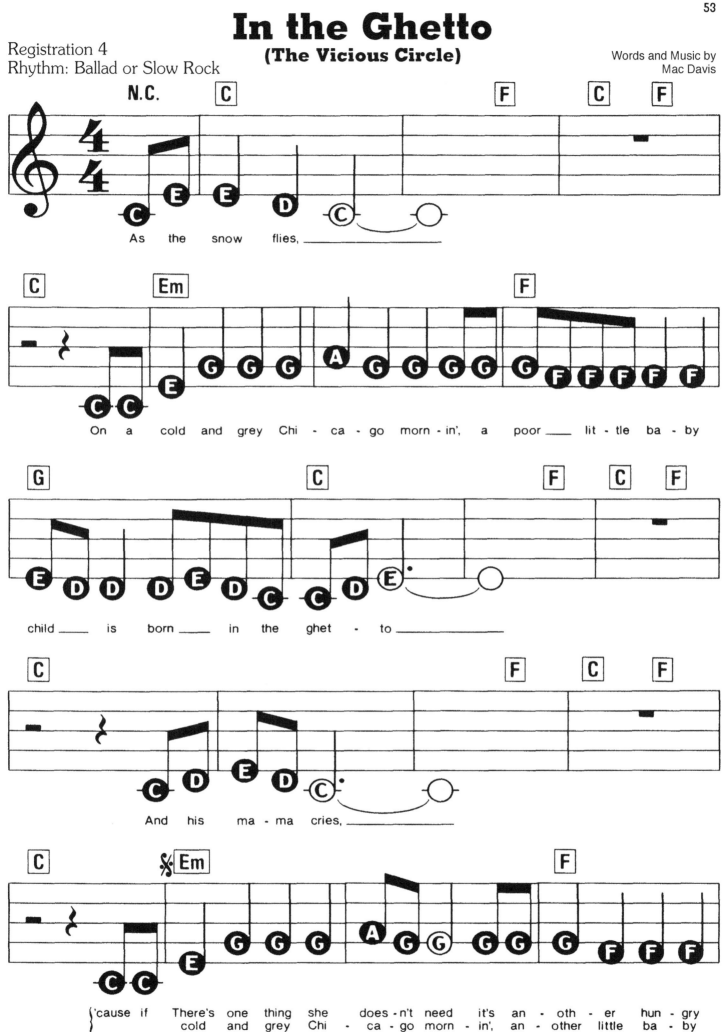

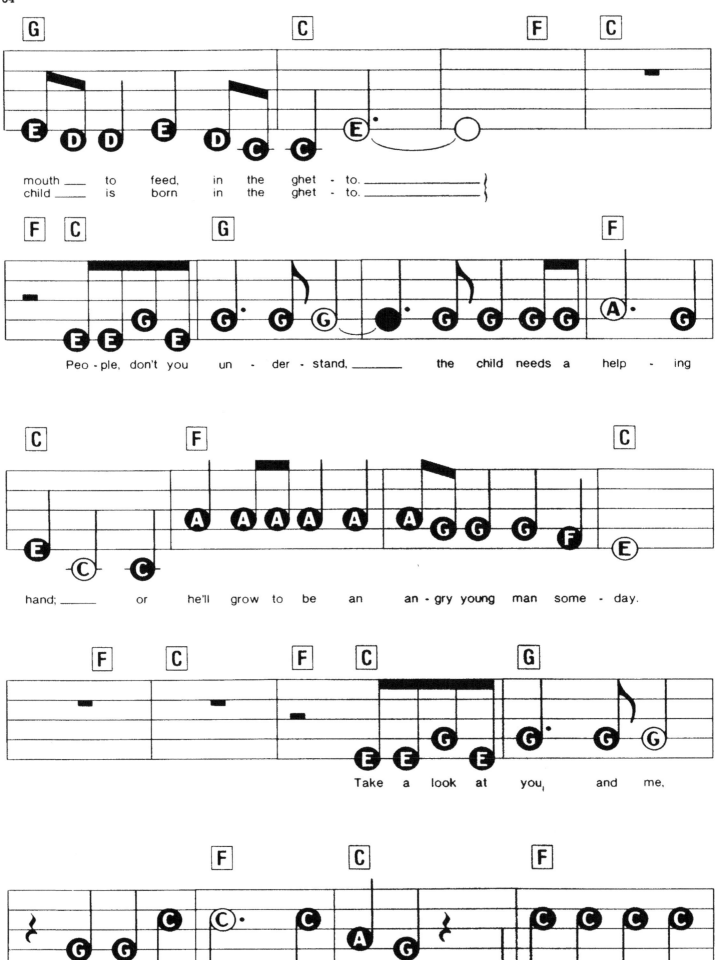

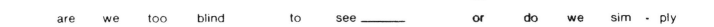

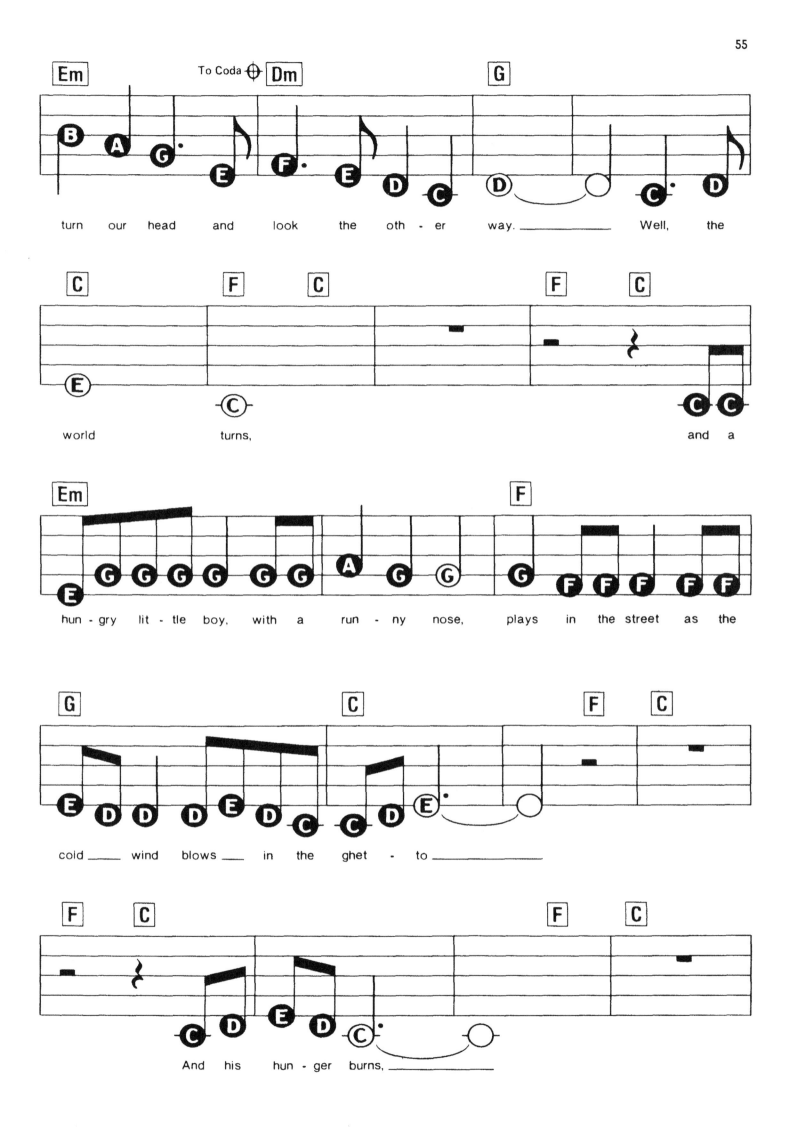

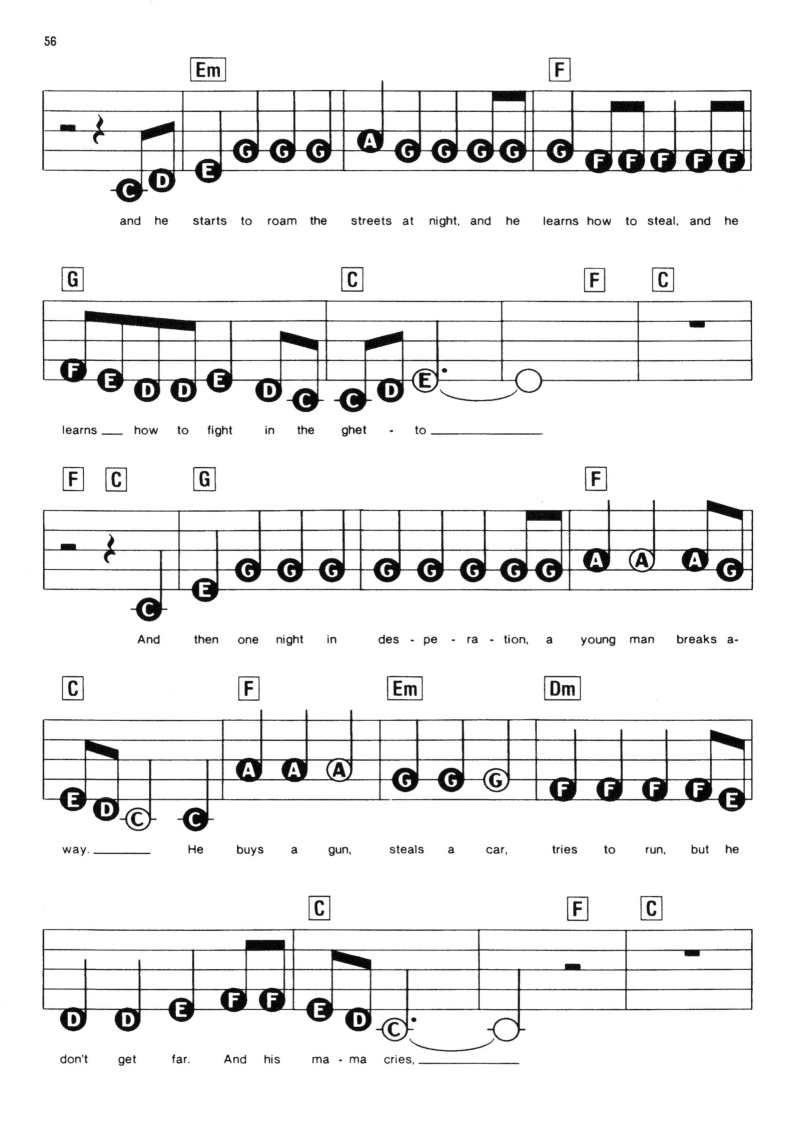

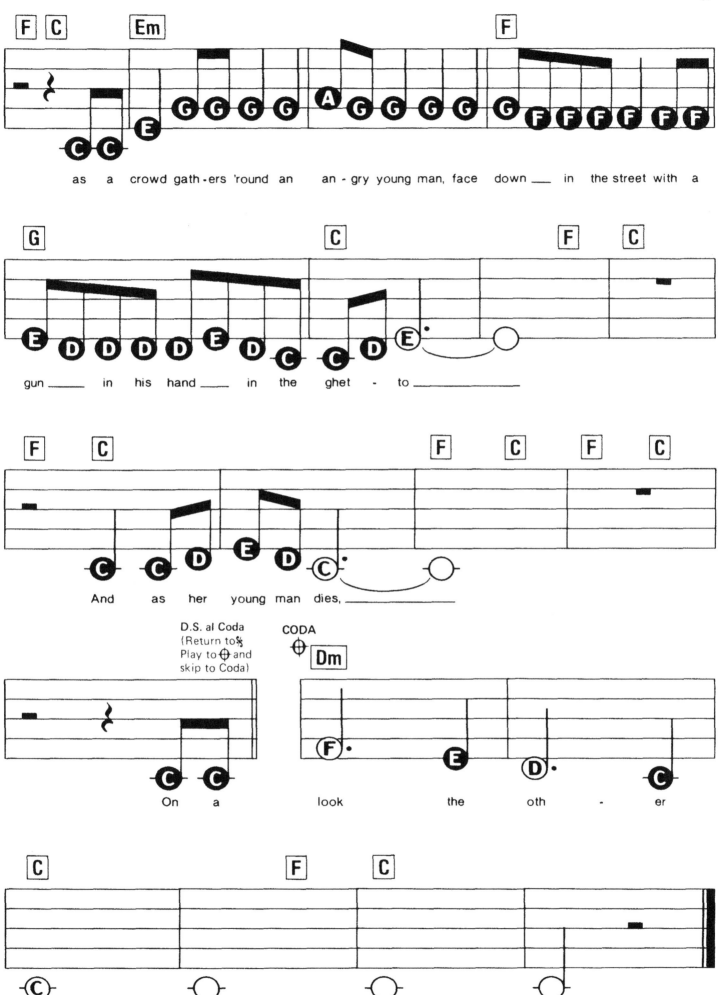

I Need Your Love Tonight

Registration 5
Rhythm: Rock

Words and Music by Sid Wayne
and Bix Reichner

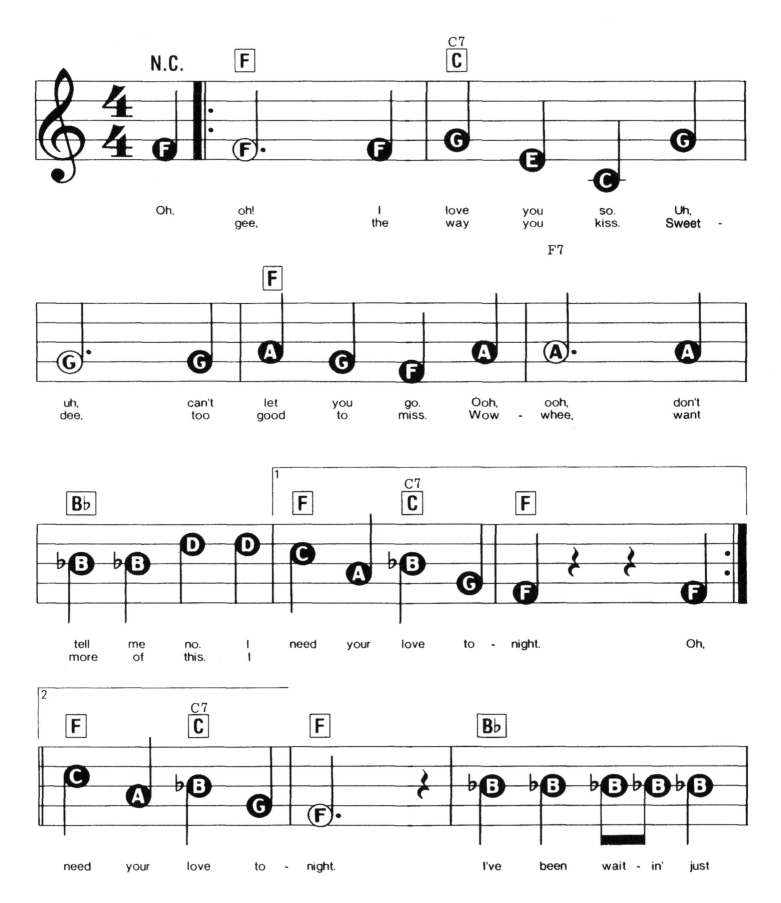

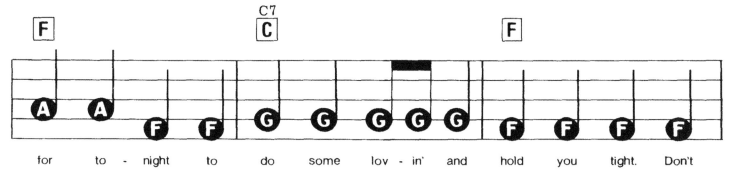

for to - night to do some lov - in' and hold you tight. Don't

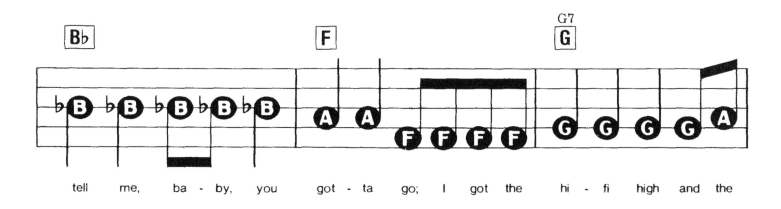

tell me, ba - by, you got - ta go; I got the hi - fi high and the

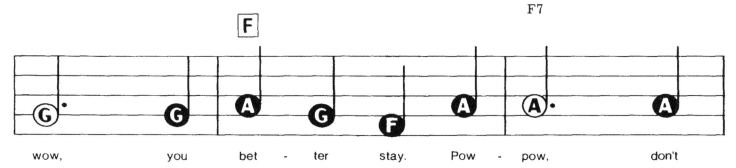

lights down low. Hey, now, hear what I say. Ooh -

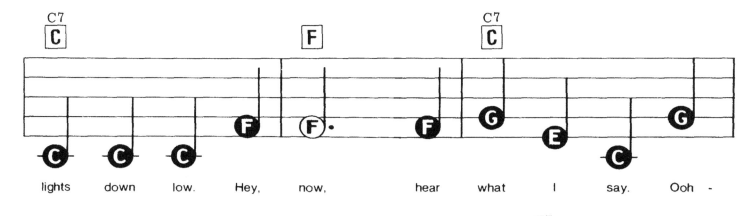

wow, you bet - ter stay. Pow - pow, don't

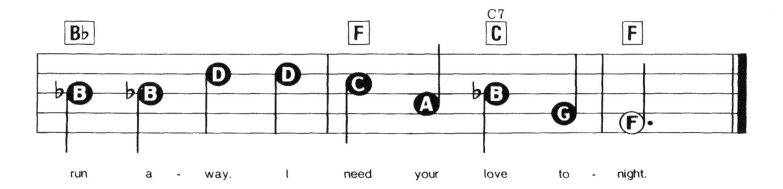

run a - way. I need your love to - night.

I Want You, I Need You, I Love You

Registration 2
Rhythm: Rock or Slow Rock

Words and Music by Maurice Mysels
and Ira Kosloff

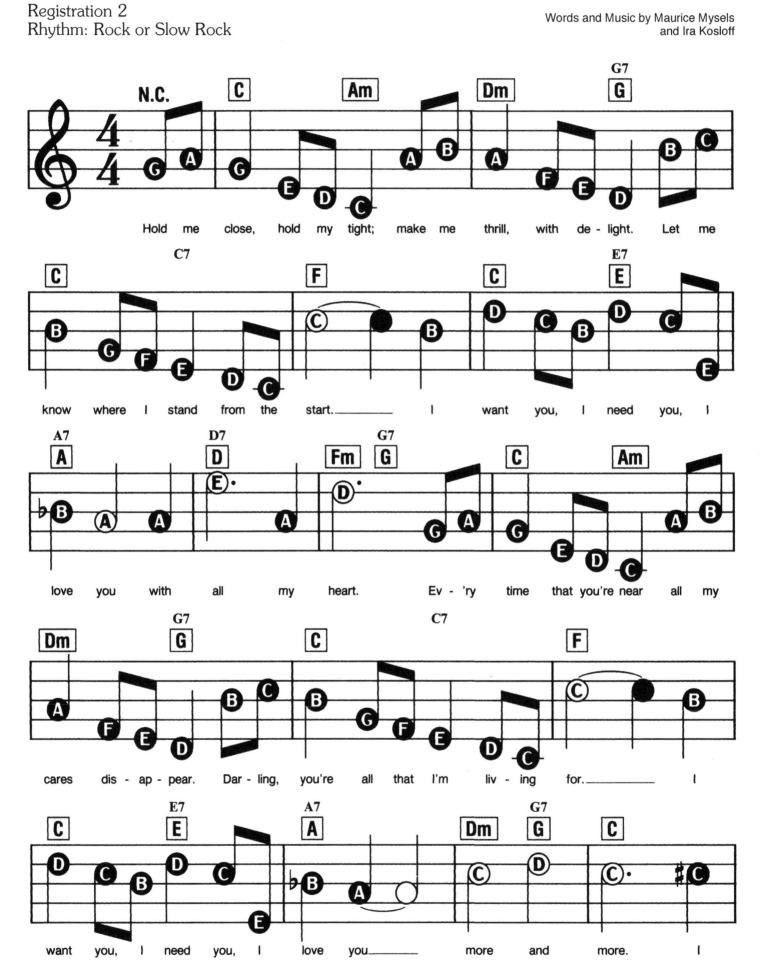

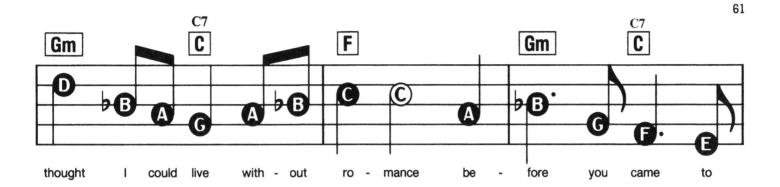

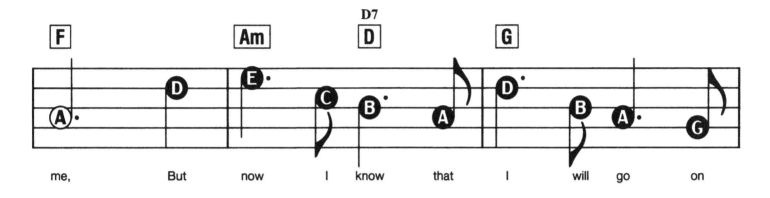

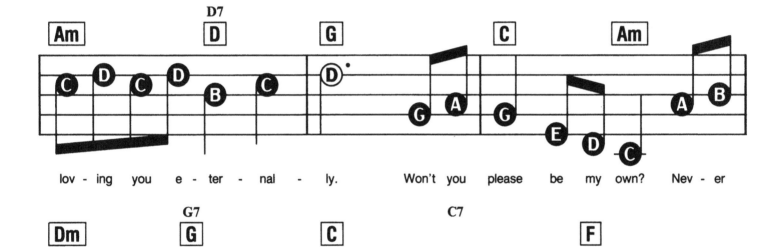

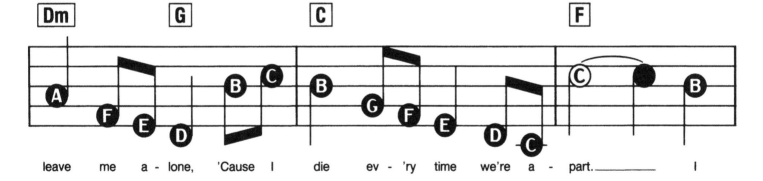

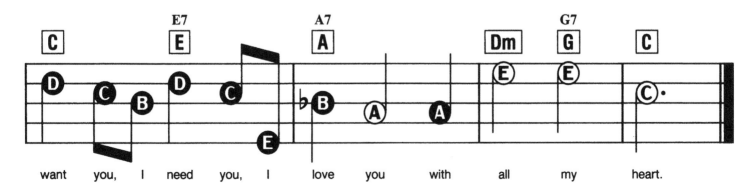

I'm Left, You're Right, She's Gone

Registration 5
Rhythm: Rock

Words and Music by Stanley A. Kesler
and William E. Taylor

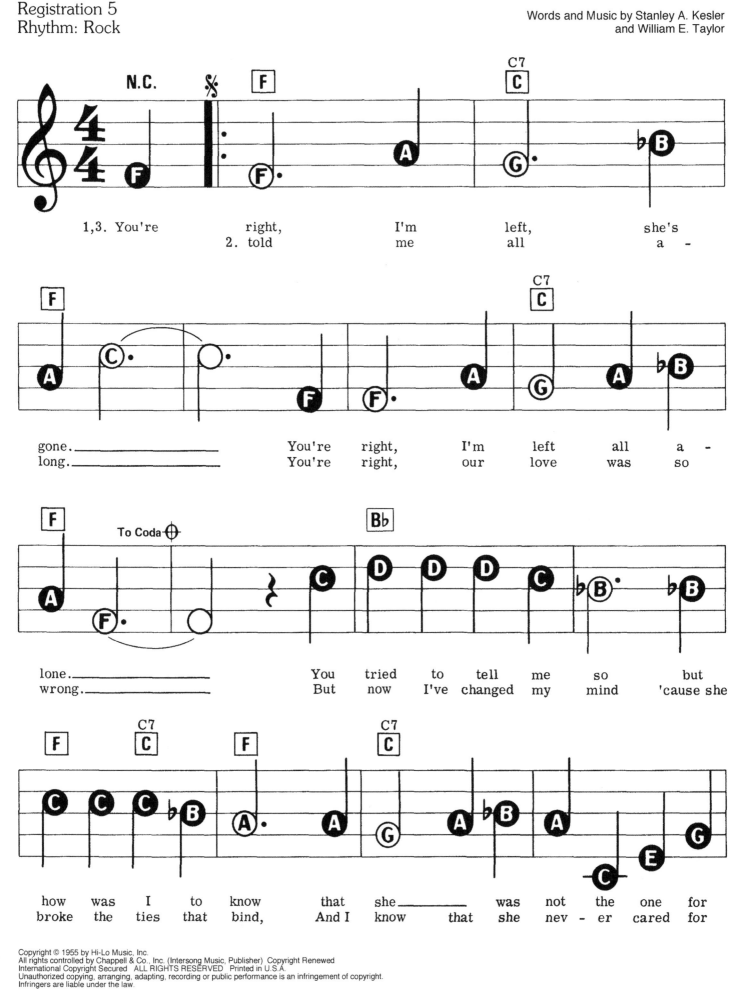

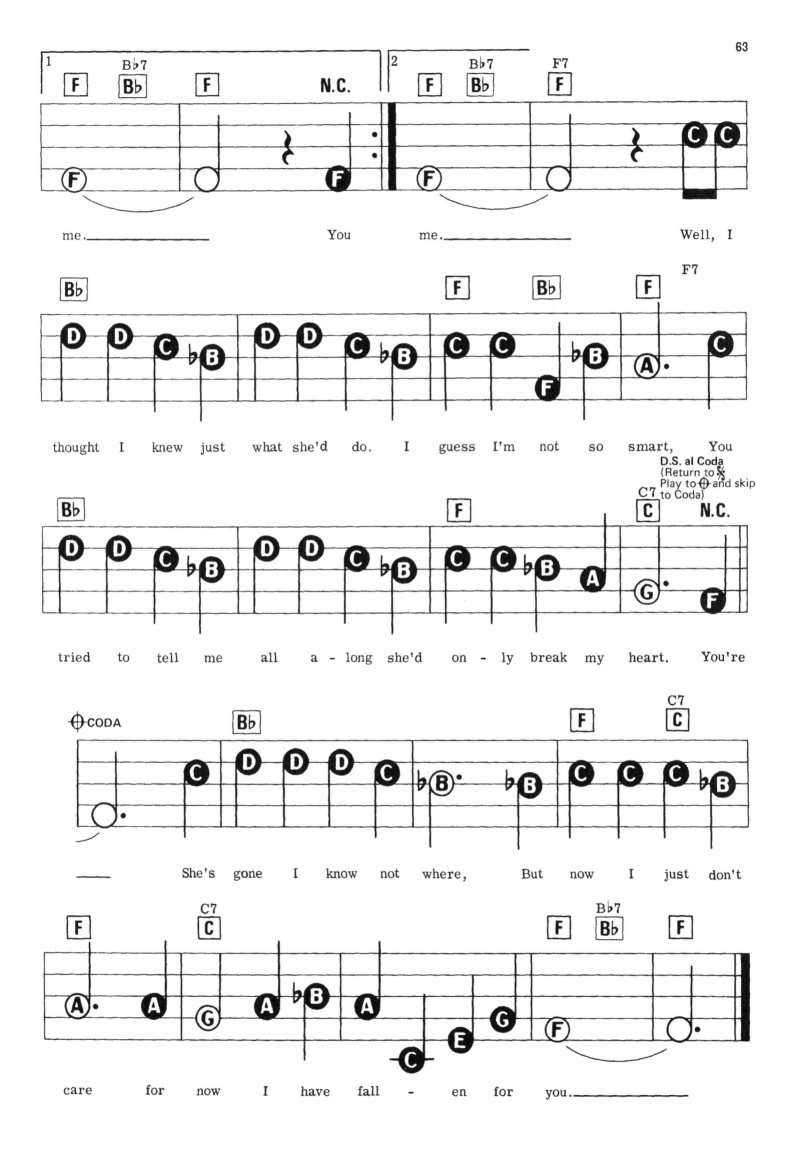

It's Now or Never

Registration 10
Rhythm: Fox Trot or Swing

Words and Music by Aaron Schroeder
and Wally Gold

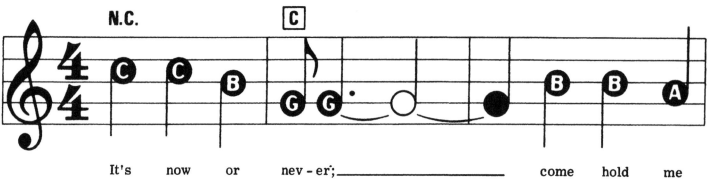

It's   now   or   nev-er;___   come   hold   me

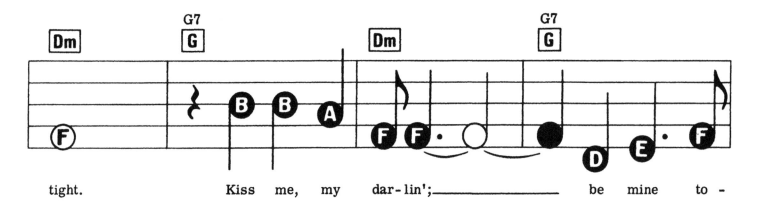

tight.   Kiss   me,   my   dar-lin';___   be   mine   to-

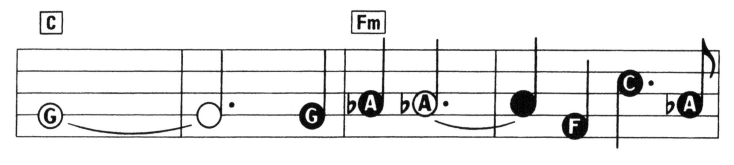

night.___   To - mor - row___   will   be   too

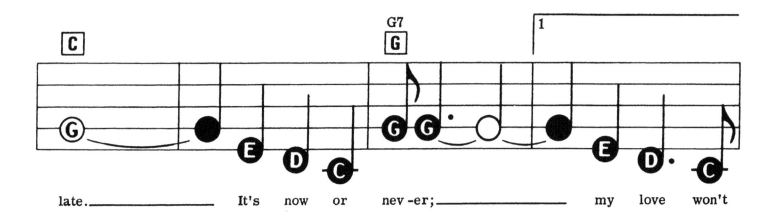

late.___   It's   now   or   nev -er;___   my   love   won't

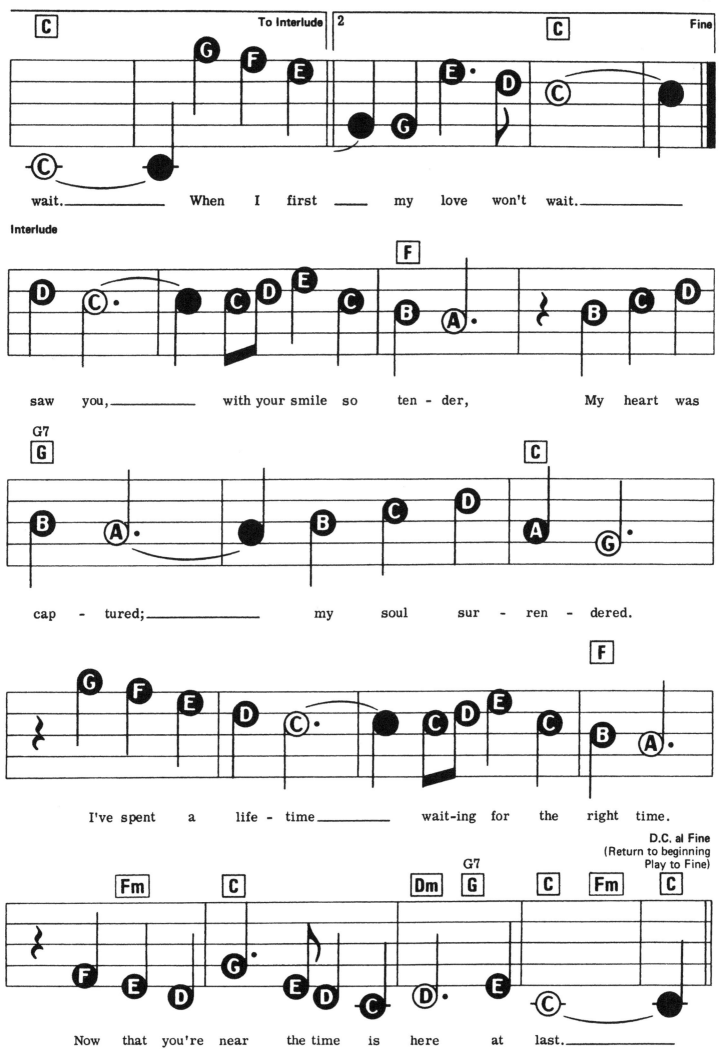

Jailhouse Rock

Registration 7
Rhythm: Rock

Words and Music by Jerry Leiber
and Mike Stoller

The ward-en threw a par-ty in the coun-ty jail. The

pris-on band was there and they be-gan to wail. The band was jump-in' and the joint be-

gan to swing. You should-'ve heard those knocked out jail-birds sing. Let's

rock! Let's rock! Ev-'ry-

bod-y in the whole cell block was a-danc-in' to the Jail-house

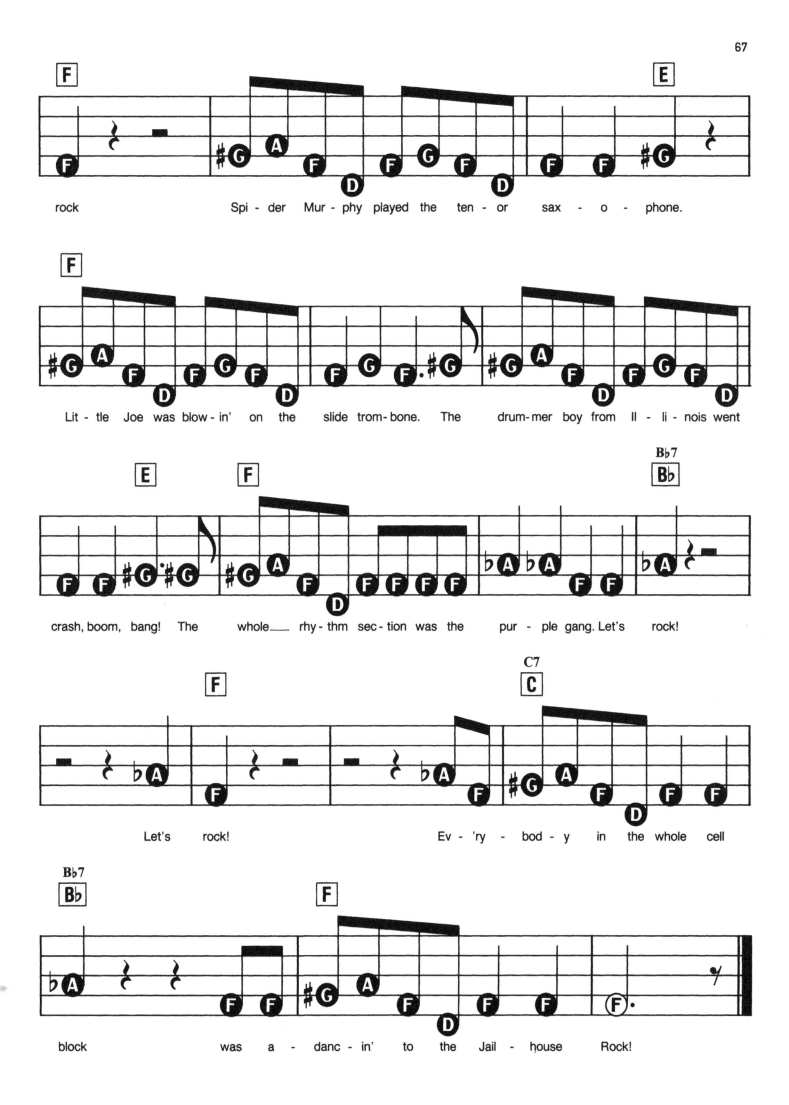

Kentucky Rain

Registration 8
Rhythm: Rock

Words and Music by Eddie Rabbitt
and Dick Heard

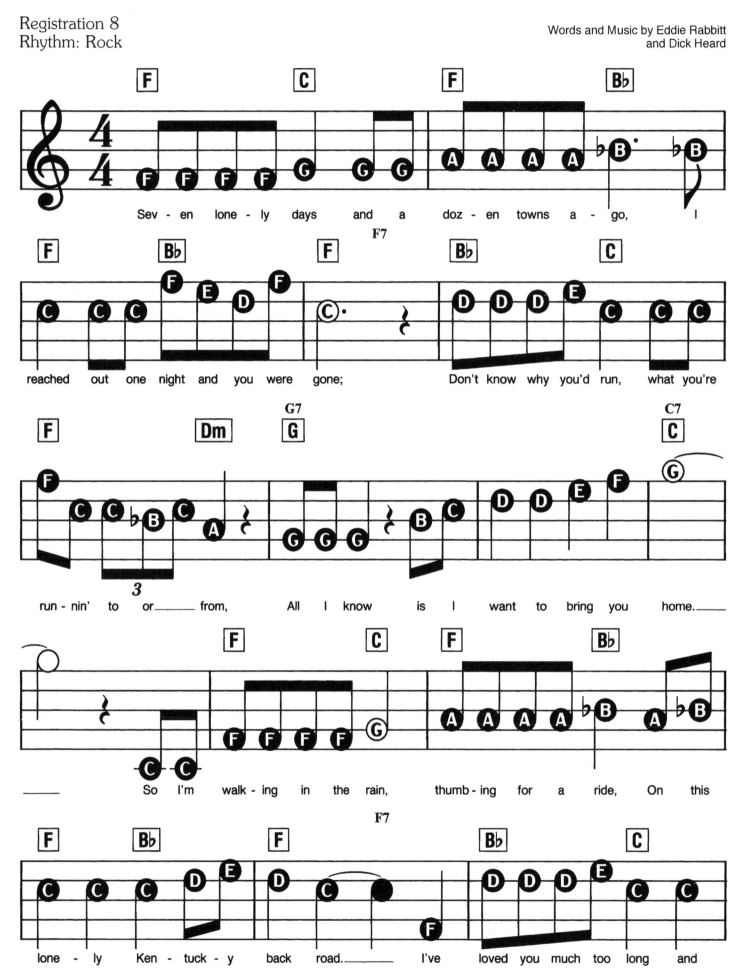

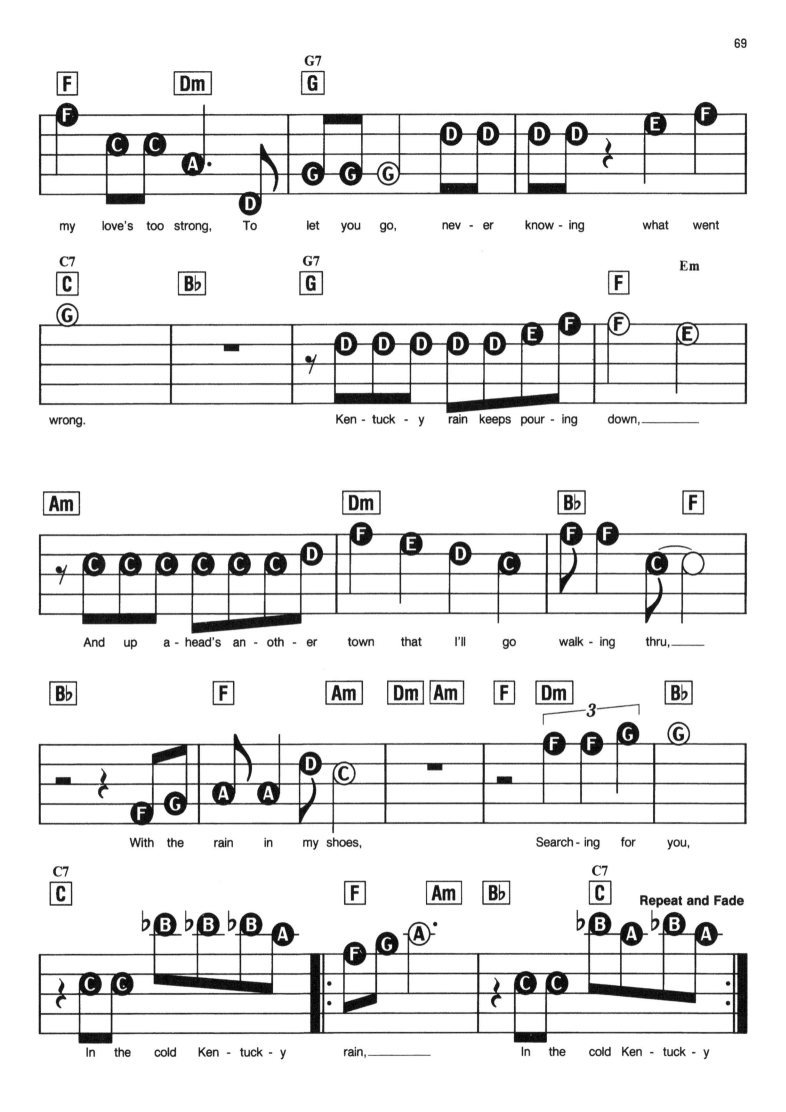

Let It Be Me
(Je t'appartiens)

English Words by Mann Curtis
French Words by Pierre Delanoe
Music by Gilbert Becaud

Registration 8
Rhythm: Ballad

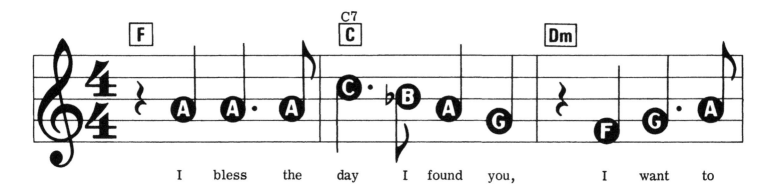

I bless the day I found you, I want to

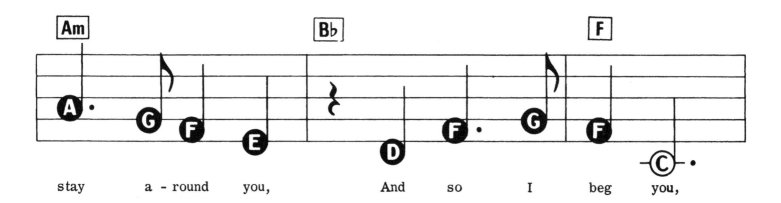

stay a - round you, And so I beg you,

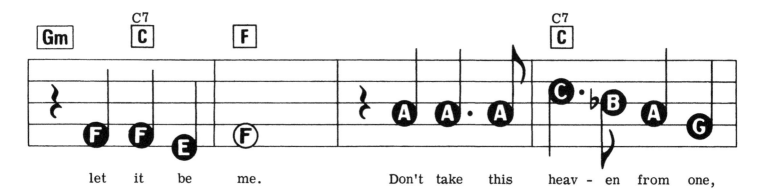

let it be me. Don't take this heav - en from one,

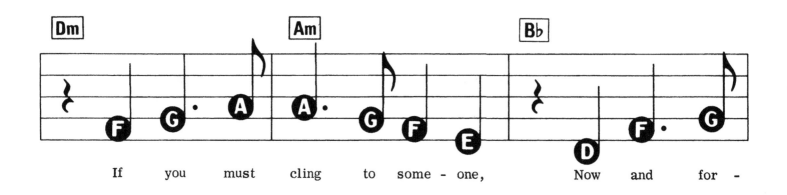

If you must cling to some - one, Now and for -

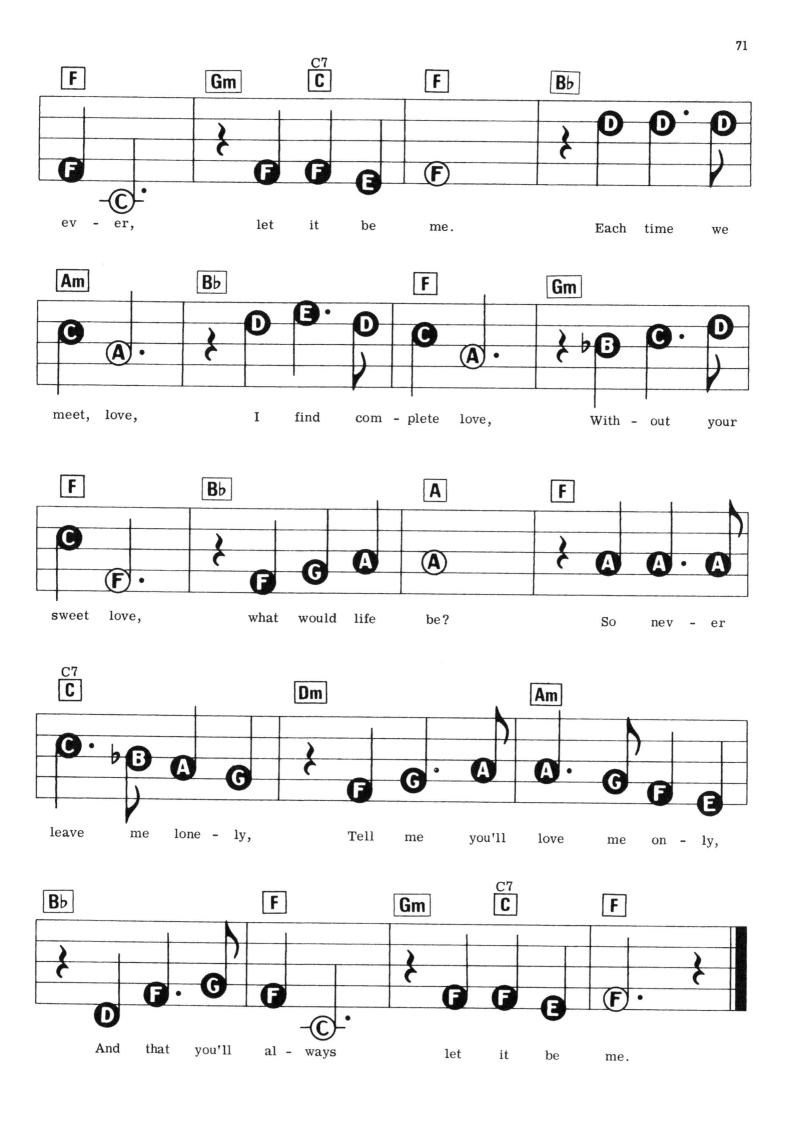

Love Me

Registration 2
Rhythm: Rock

Words and Music by Jerry Leiber
and Mike Stoller

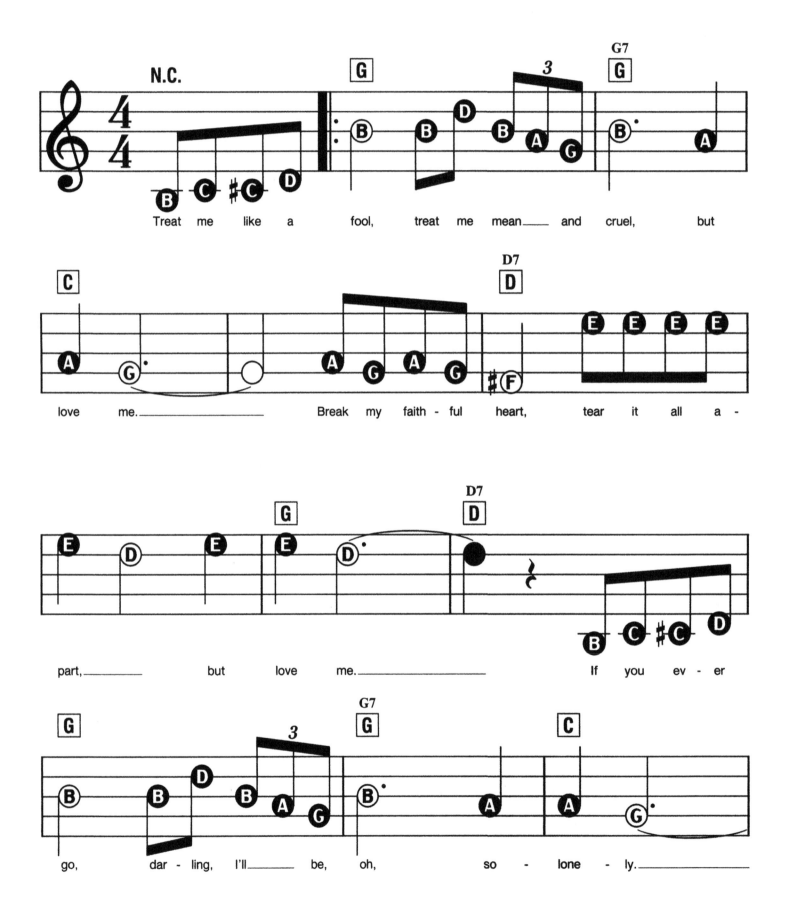

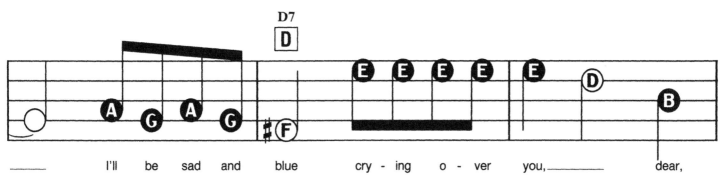

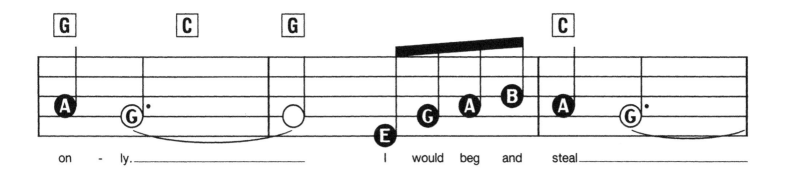

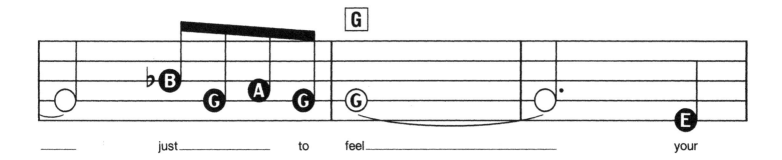

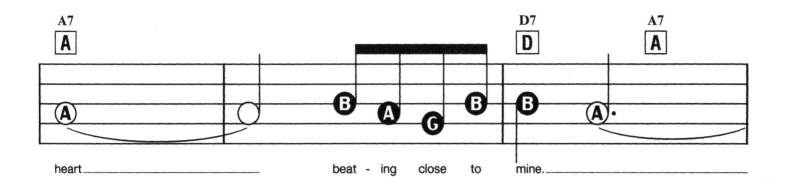

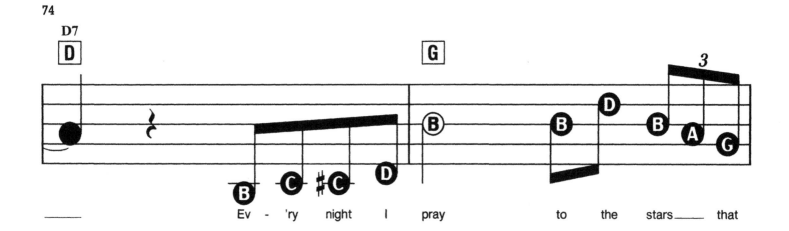

Ev - 'ry night I pray to the stars_____ that

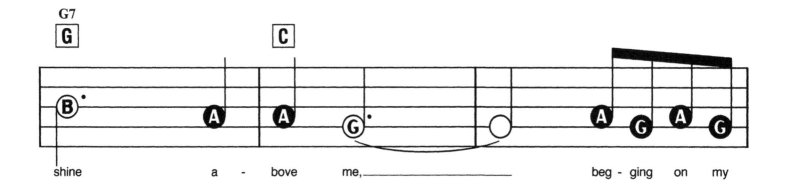

shine a - bove me,_____ beg - ging on my

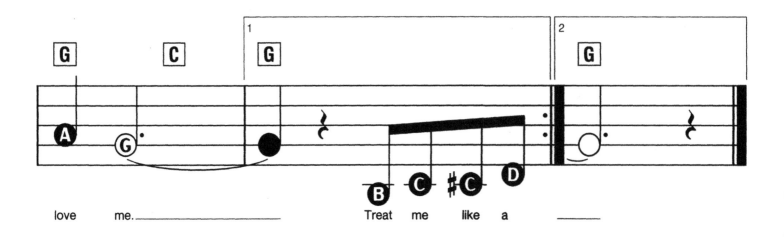

knees, all I ask is please,_____ please,

love me._____ Treat me like a _____

Moody Blue

Registration 1
Rhythm: Rock

Words and Music by
Mark James

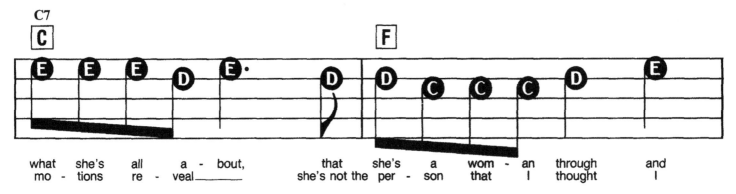

what she's all a - bout, that she's a wom - an through and
mo - tions re - veal___ she's not the per - son that I thought I

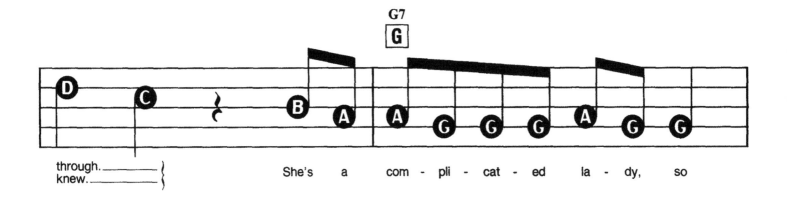

through.___ } She's a com - pli - cat - ed la - dy, so
knew.___ }

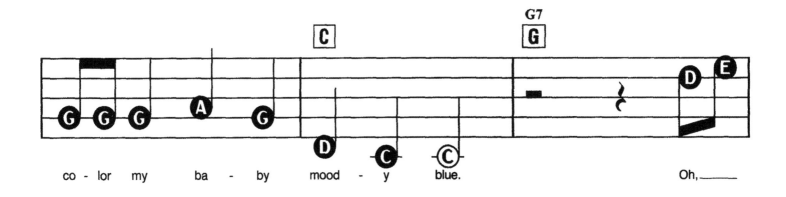

co - lor my ba - by mood - y blue. Oh,___

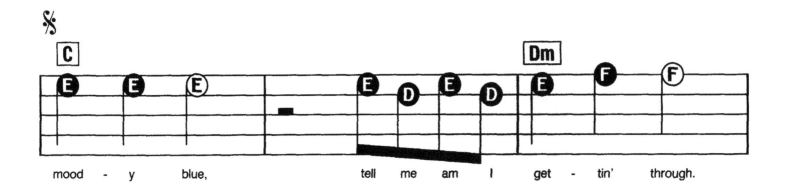

mood - y blue, tell me am I get - tin' through.

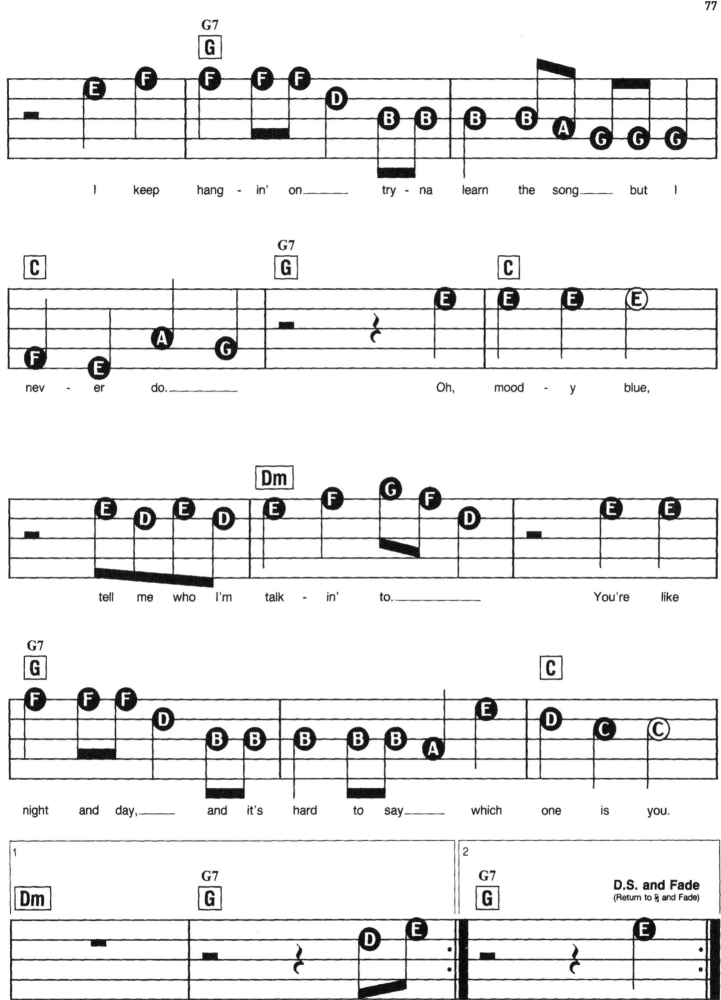

Love Me Tender

Registration 9
Rhythm: Slow Rock or Rock

Words and Music by Elvis Presley
and Vera Matson

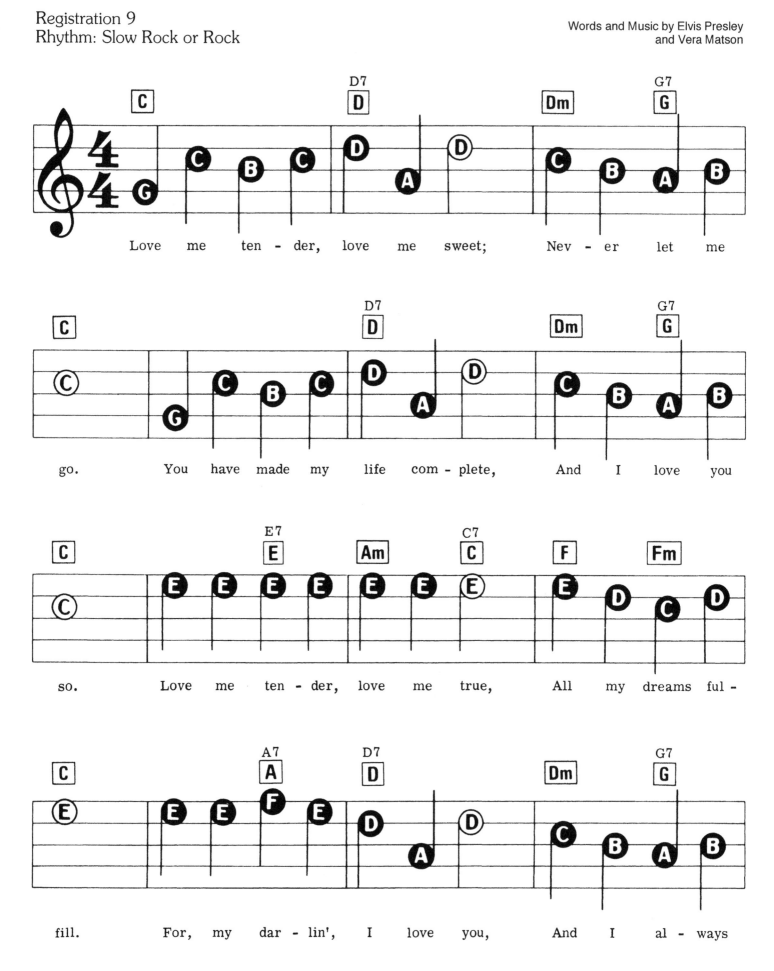

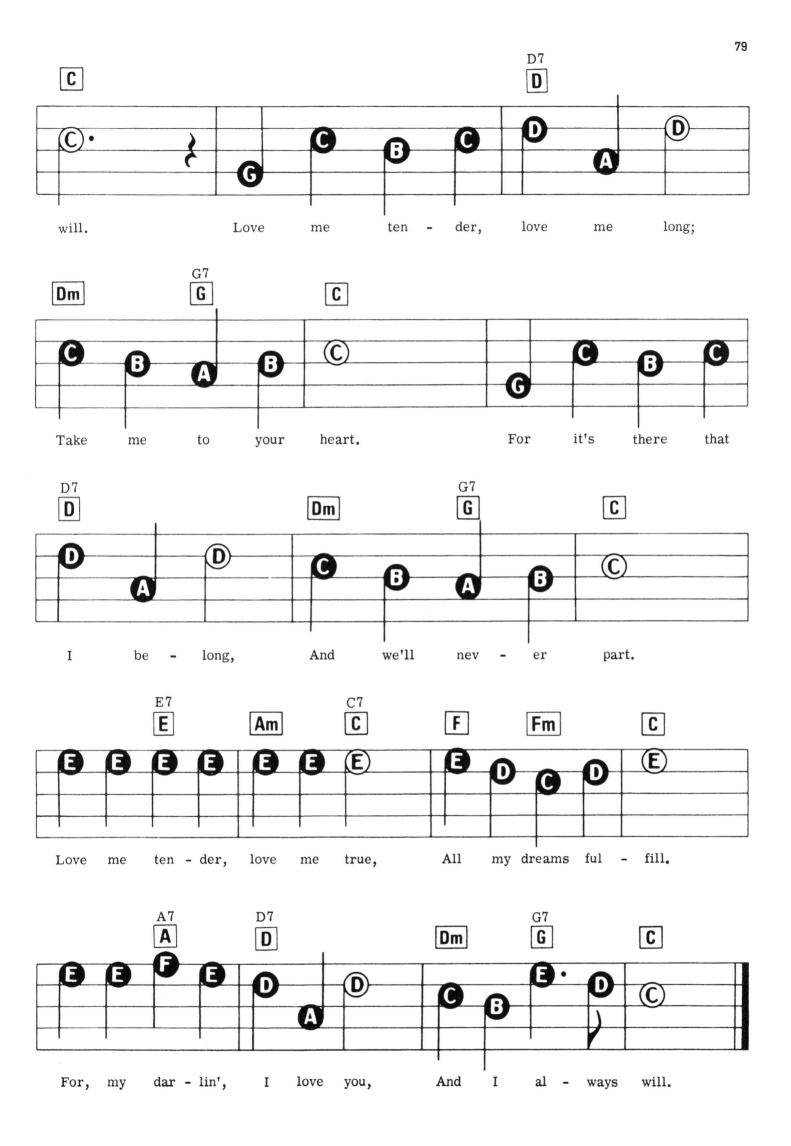

Loving You

Registration 4
Rhythm: Ballad or Slow Rock

Words and Music by Jerry Leiber
and Mike Stoller

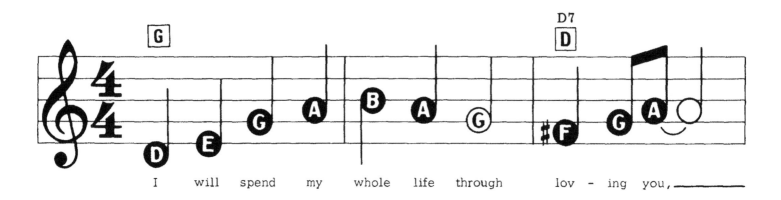

I will spend my whole life through lov - ing you, _____

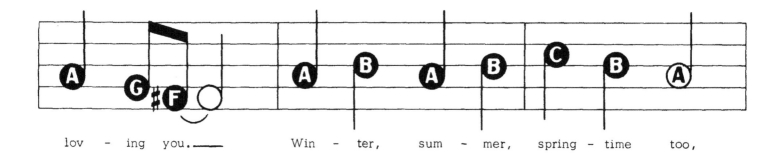

lov - ing you. _____ Win - ter, sum - mer, spring - time too,

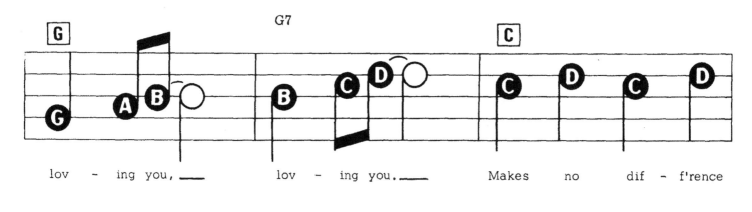

lov - ing you, _____ lov - ing you. _____ Makes no dif - f'rence

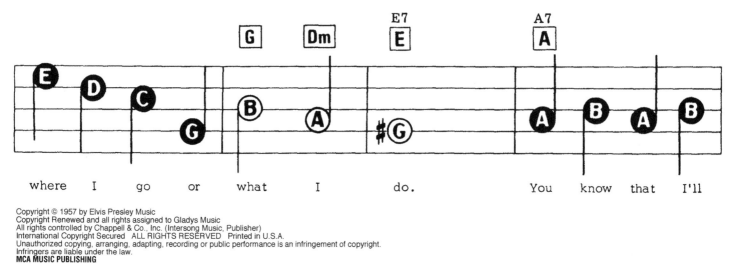

where I go or what I do. You know that I'll

MCA MUSIC PUBLISHING

81

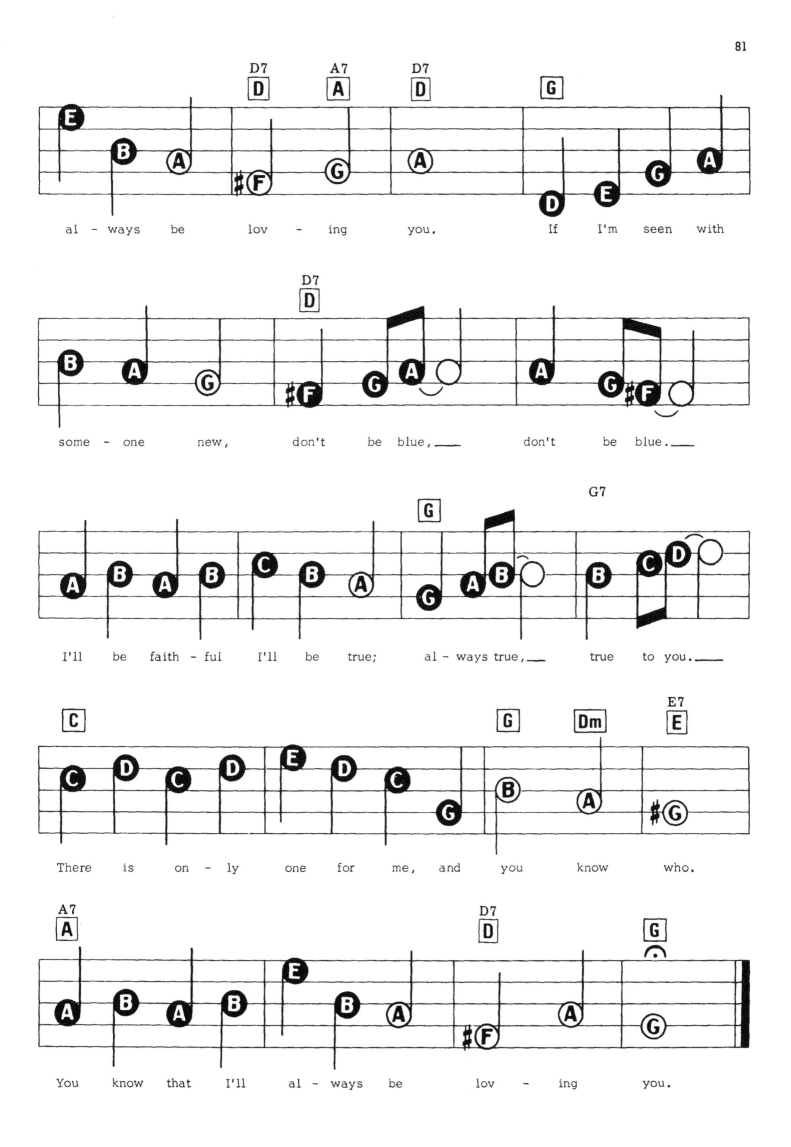

Memories

Registration 2
Rhythm: Rock

Words and Music by Billy Strange
and Scott Davis

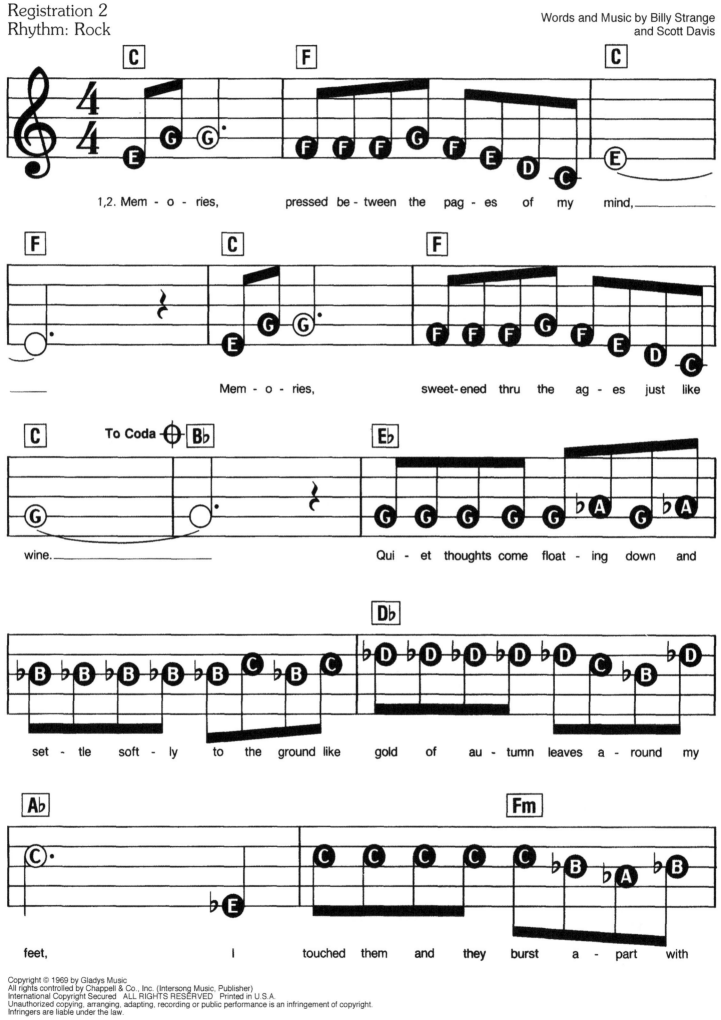

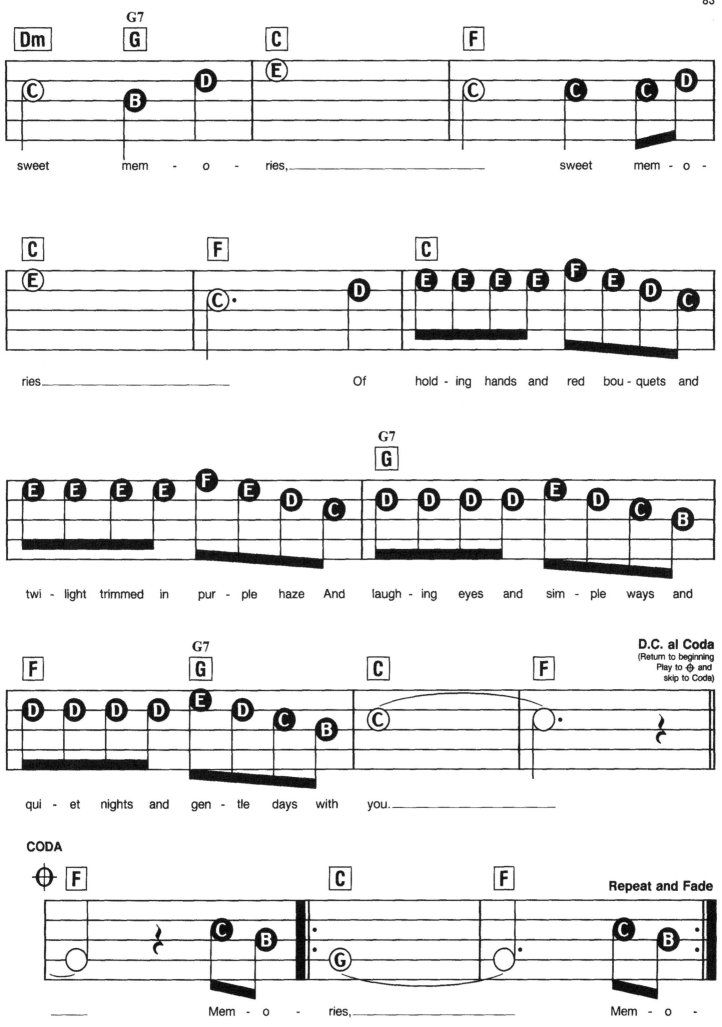

My Baby Left Me

Registration 10
Rhythm: Rock

Words and Music by
Arthur Crudup

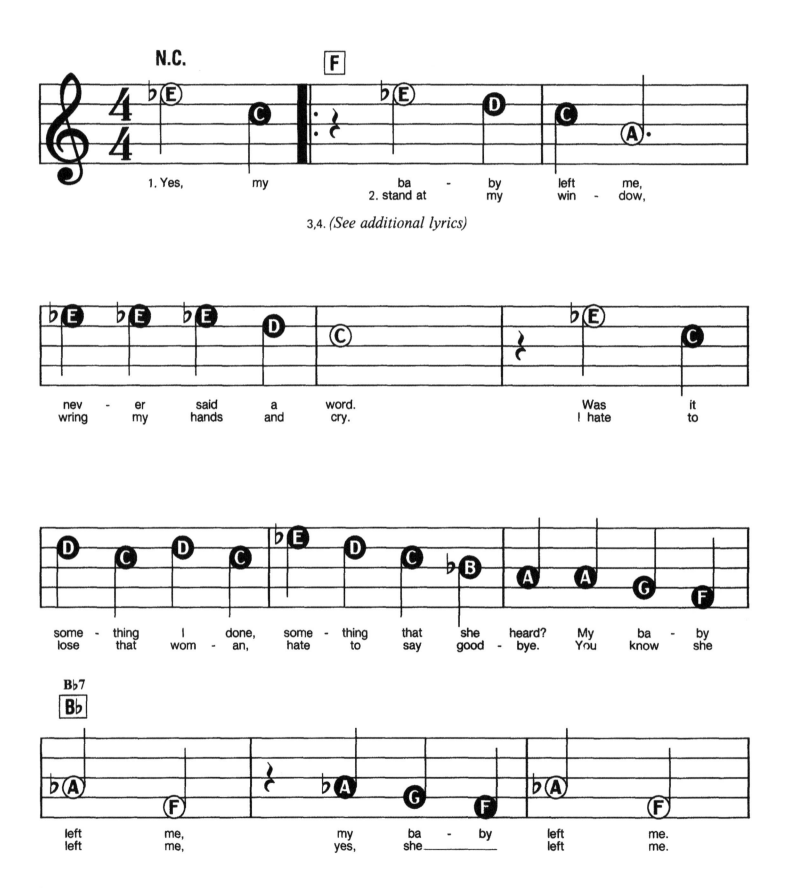

3,4. *(See additional lyrics)*

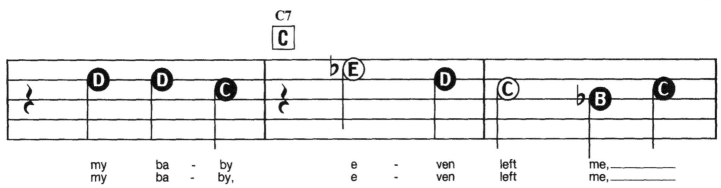

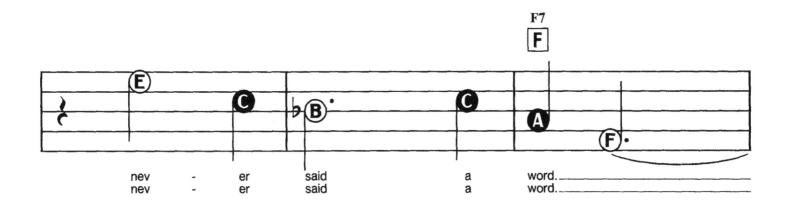

my ba - by ___ e - ven left me,_____
my ba - by, ___ e - ven left me,_____

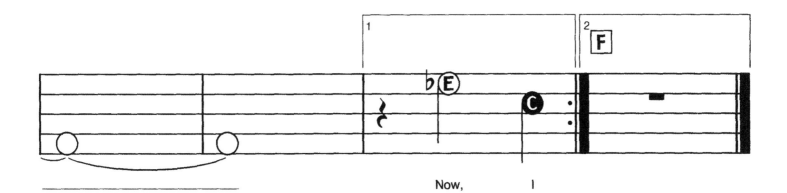

nev - er said ___ a word._____
nev - er said ___ a word._____

Now, I

Additional Lyrics

3. Baby, one of these mornings, Lord, it won't be long,
You'll look for me and, Baby, and Daddy he'll be gone.
You know you left me, you know you left me.
My baby even left me, never said goodbye.

4. Now, I stand at my window, wring my hands and moan.
All I know is that the one I love is gone.
My baby left me, you know she left me.
My baby even left me, never said a word.

My Way

Registration 5
Rhythm: Ballad or Rock

English Words by Paul Anka
Original French Words by Gilles Thibault
Music by Jacques Revaux and Claude Francois

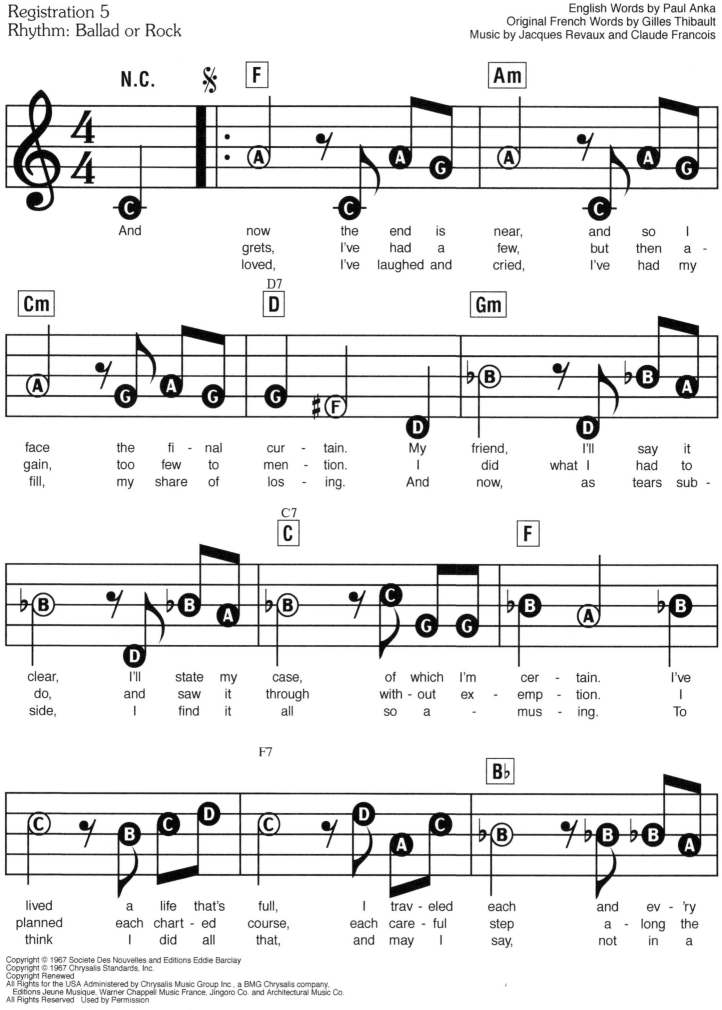

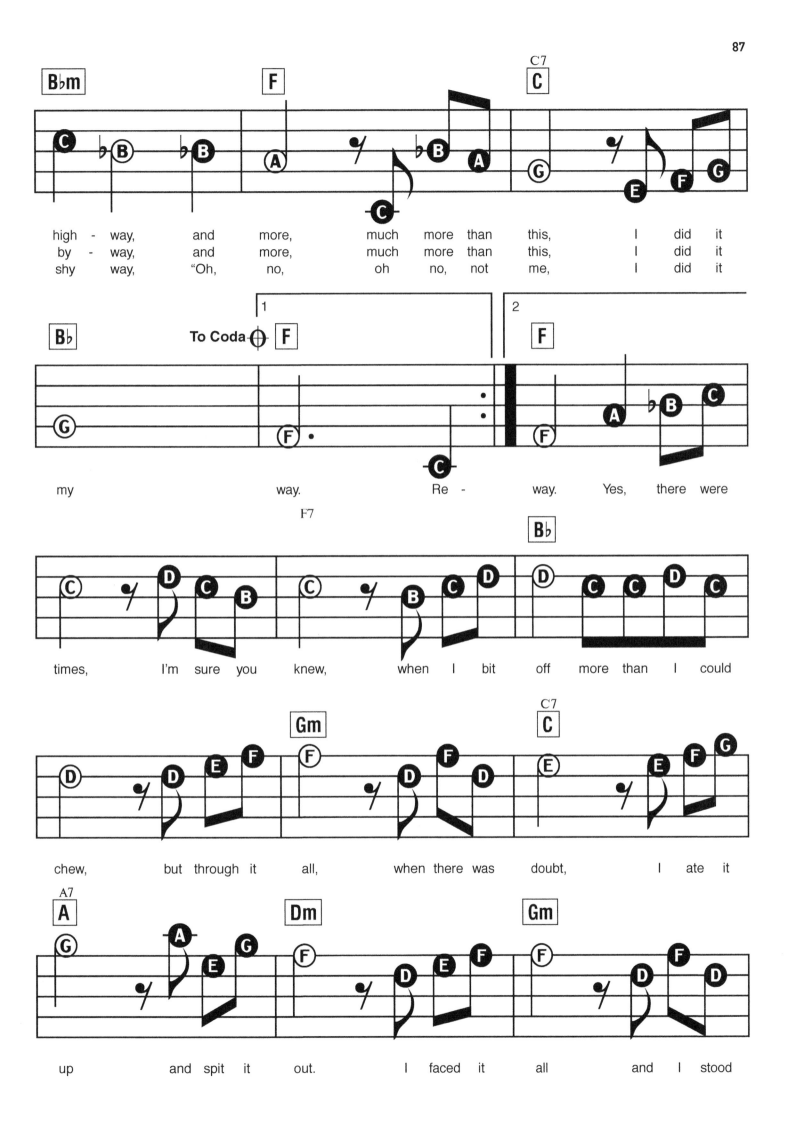

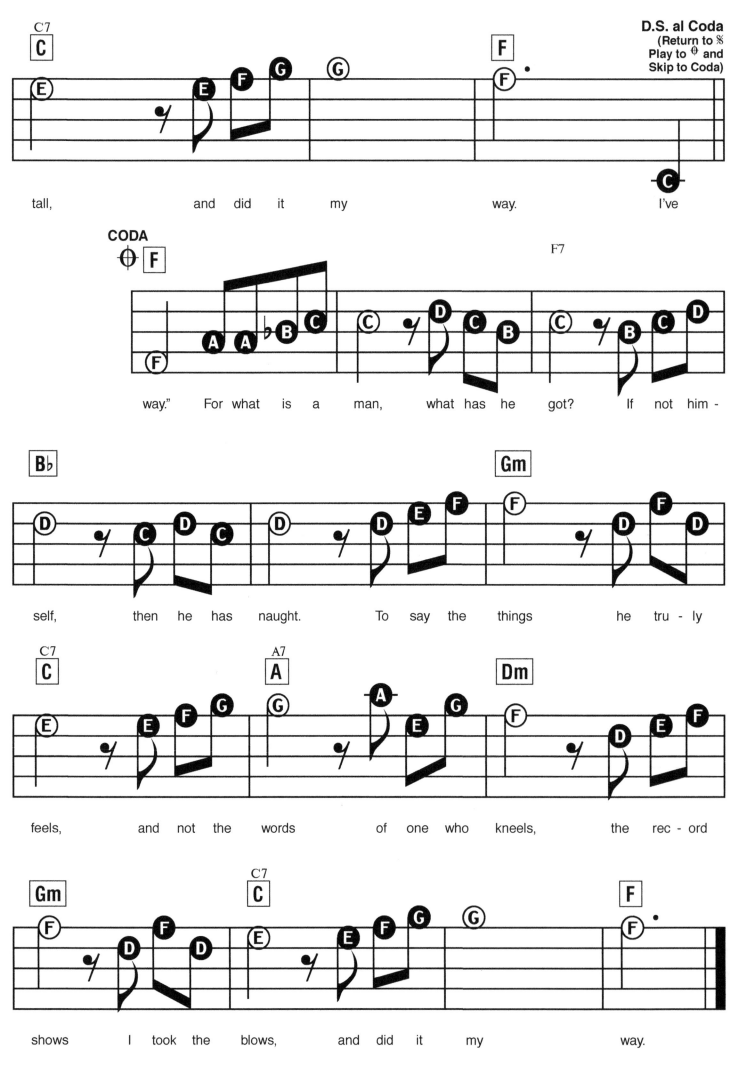

D.S. al Coda
(Return to 𝄋
Play to ⊕ and
Skip to Coda)

tall,   and did it my   way.   I've

CODA

way." For what is a man, what has he got? If not him -

self,   then he has naught. To say the things he tru - ly

feels,   and not the words of one who kneels, the rec - ord

shows   I took the blows, and did it my   way.

Old Shep

Registration 9
Rhythm: Waltz

Words and Music by
Clyde (Red) Foley

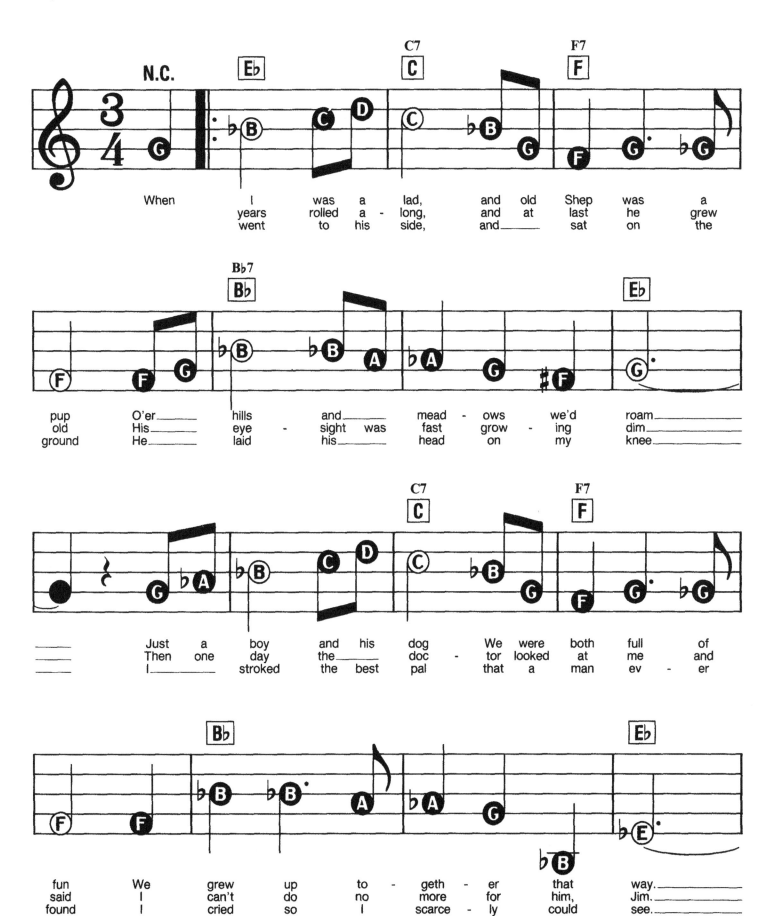

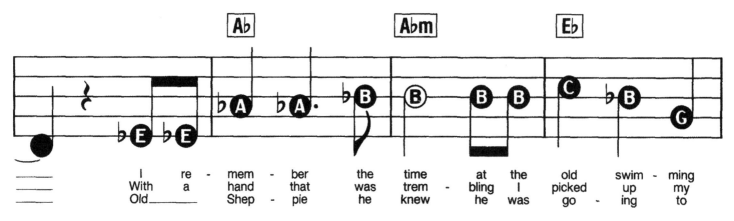

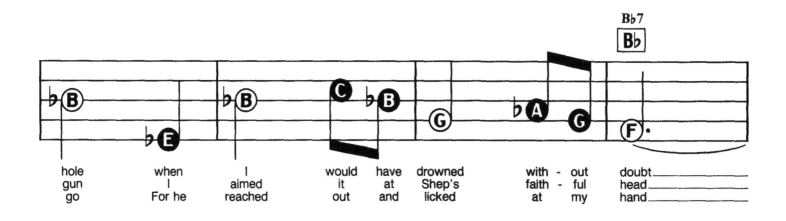

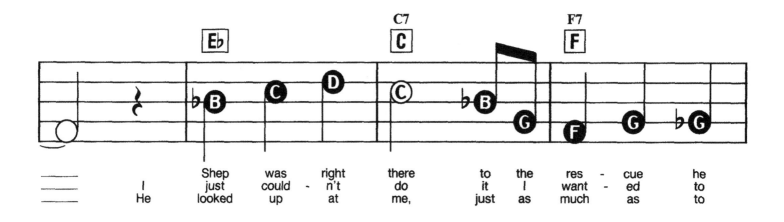

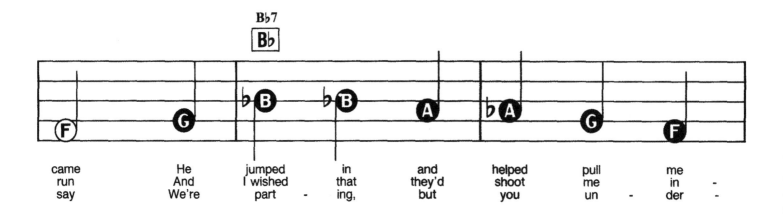

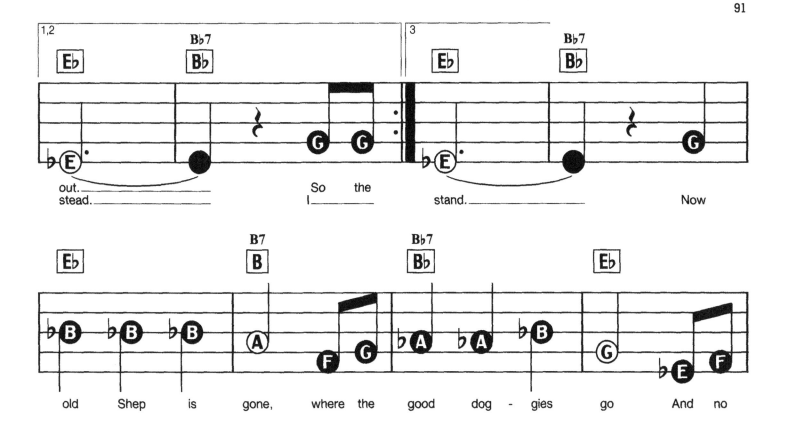

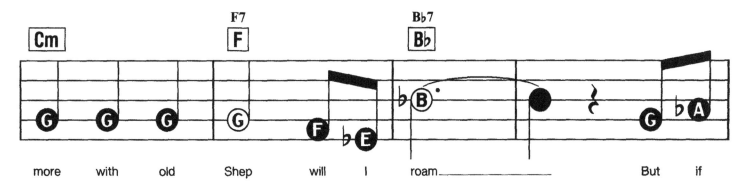

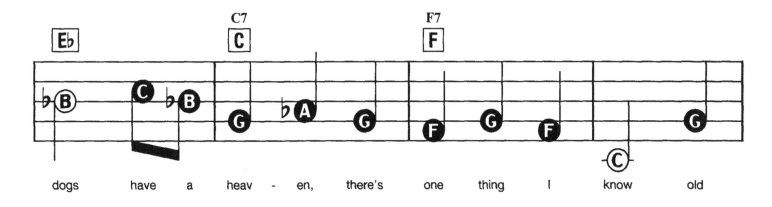

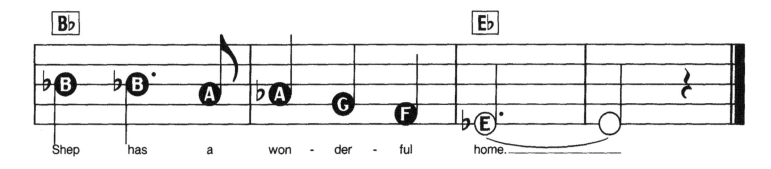

(There Will Be)
Peace in the Valley
(for Me)

Registration 2
Rhythm: Waltz

Words and Music by
Thomas A. Dorsey

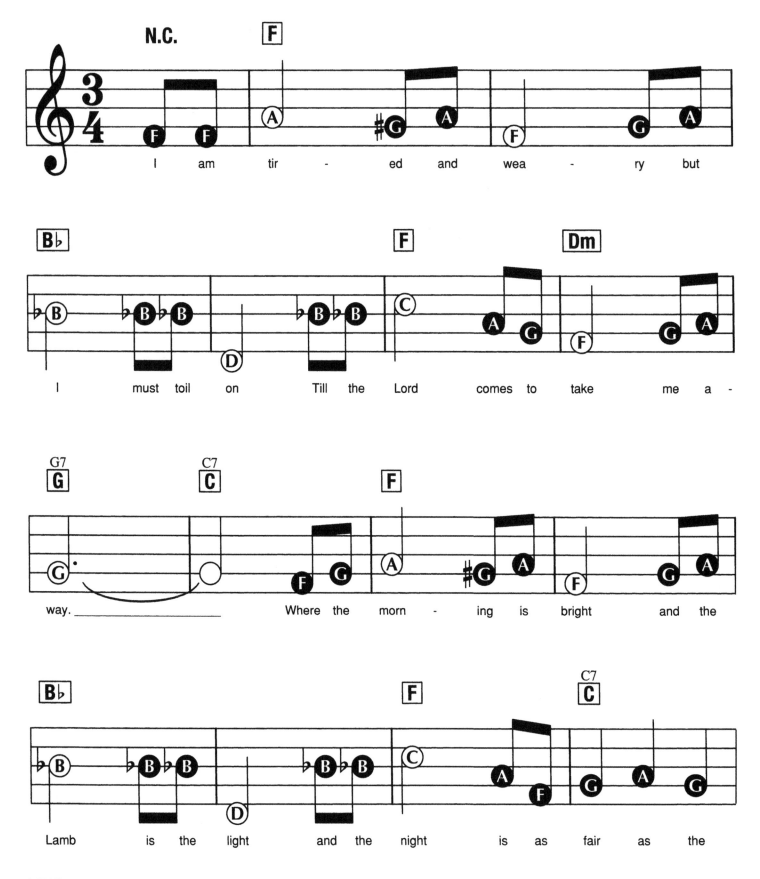

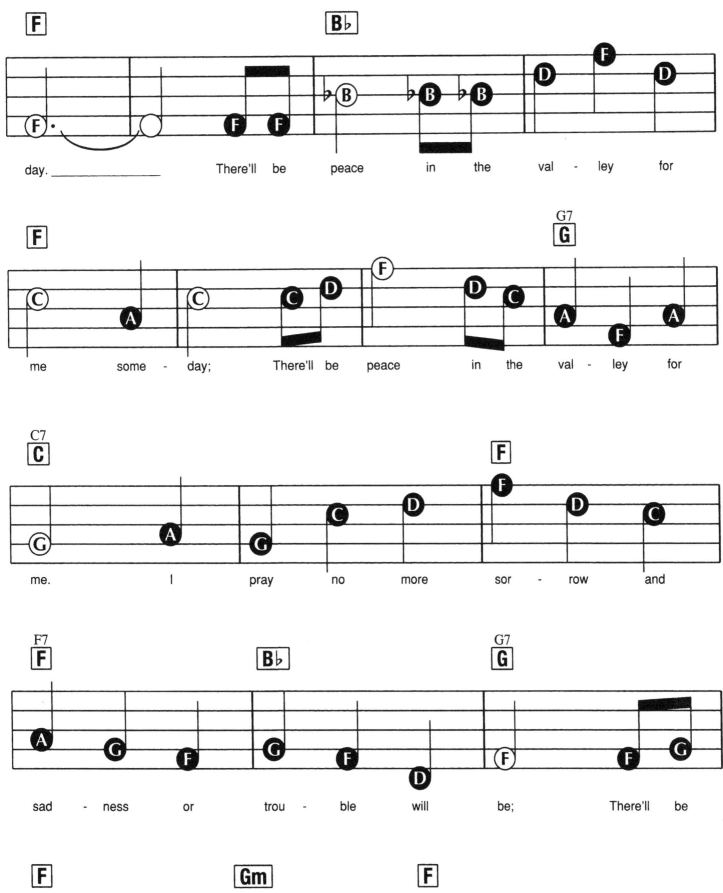

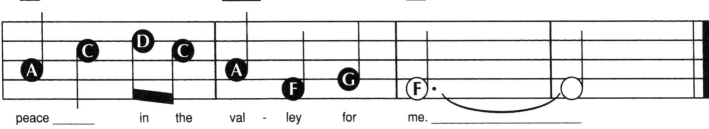

Ready Teddy

Registration 6
Rhythm: Rock

Words and Music by John Marascalo
and Robert Blackwell

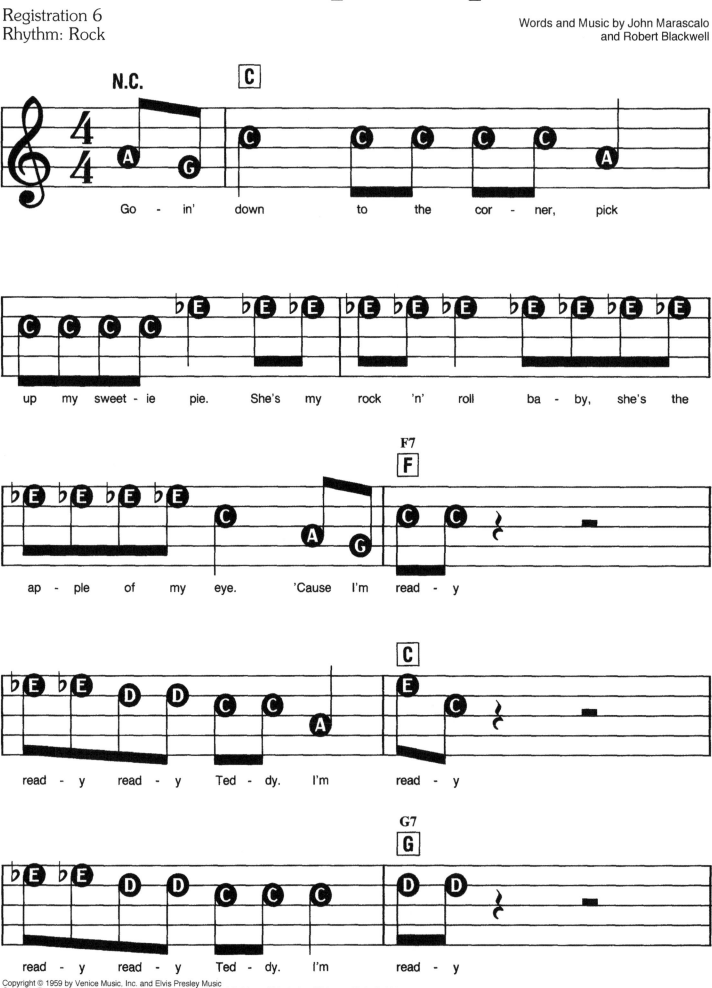

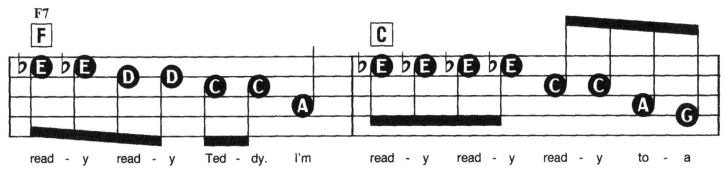

read-y read-y Ted-dy. I'm ready ready ready to a

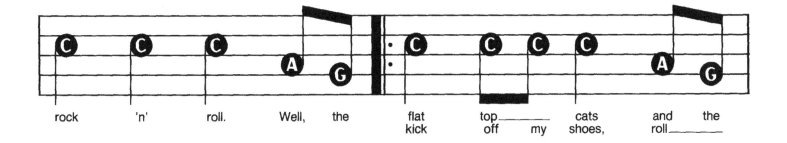

rock 'n' roll. Well, the flat top cats and the
kick off my shoes, roll

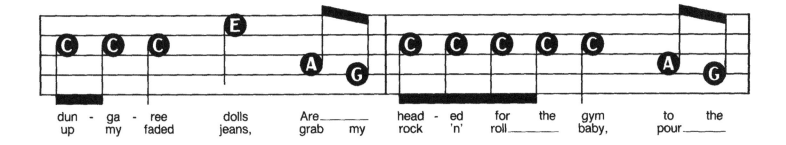

dun-ga-ree dolls Are headed for the gym to the
up my faded jeans, grab my rock 'n' roll baby, pour

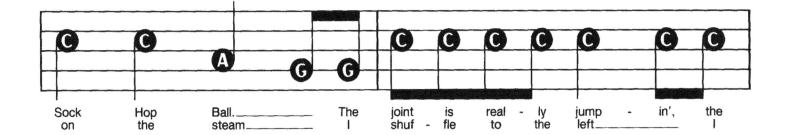

Sock Hop Ball. The joint is real-ly jump-in', the
on the steam I shuf-fle to the left I

cats are go-in' wild. The mu-sic real-ly sends me. I
shuf-fle to the right. Gonna rock 'n' roll me till the

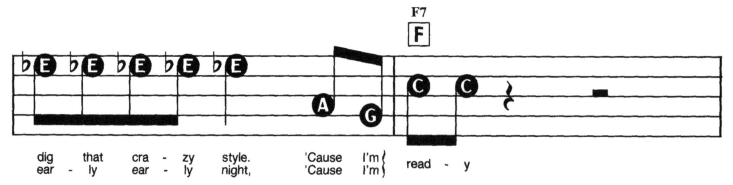

dig that cra - zy style. 'Cause I'm{ read - y
ear - ly ear - ly night, 'Cause I'm{ read - y

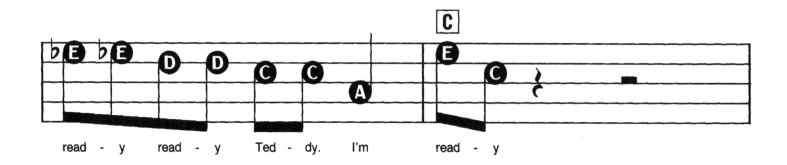

read - y read - y Ted - dy. I'm read - y

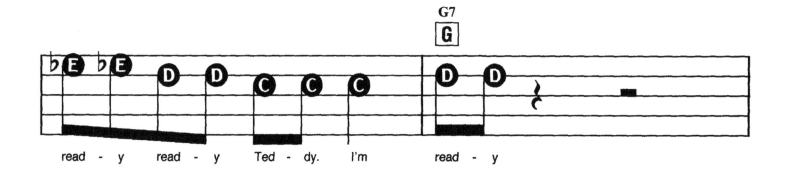

read - y read - y Ted - dy. I'm read - y

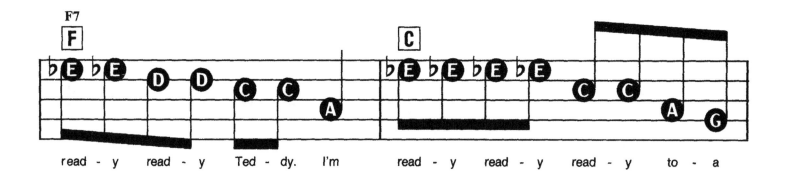

read - y read - y Ted - dy. I'm read - y read - y read - y to a

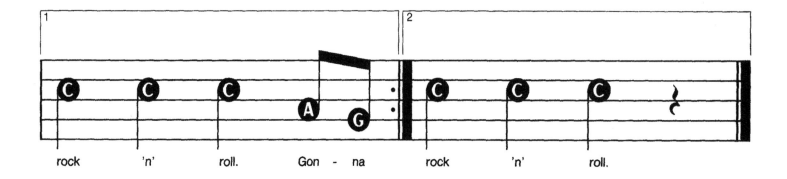

rock 'n' roll. Gon - na   rock 'n' roll.

Stuck on You

Registration 4
Rhythm: Rock

Words and Music by Aaron Schroeder
and J. Leslie McFarland

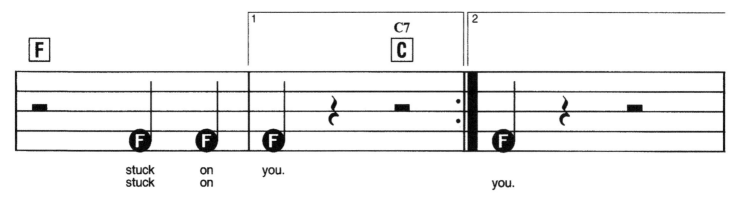

stuck on you.
stuck on you.

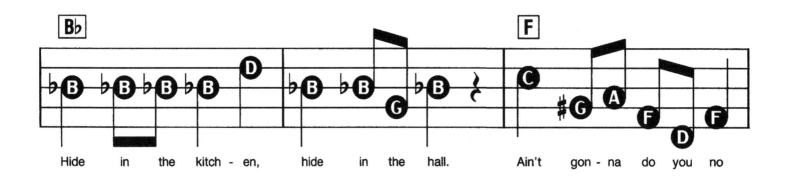

Hide in the kitch - en, hide in the hall. Ain't gon - na do you no

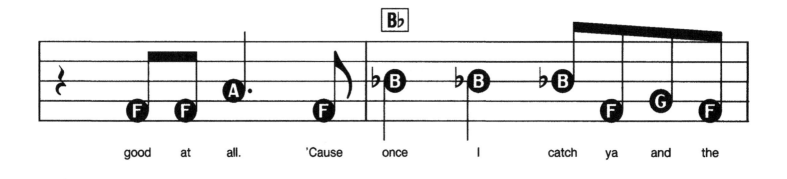

good at all. 'Cause once I catch ya and the

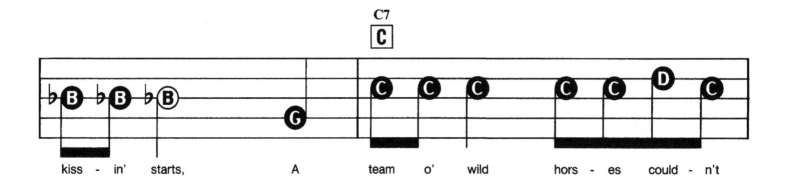

kiss - in' starts, A team o' wild hors - es could - n't

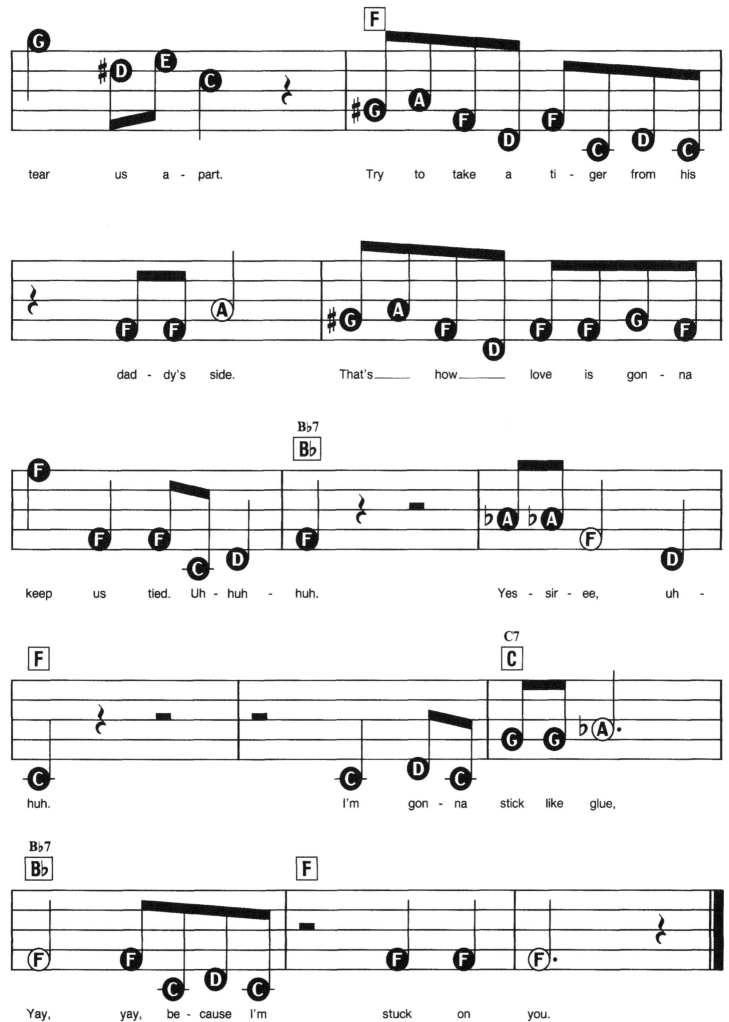

Release Me

Registration 1
Rhythm: Country

Words and Music by Robert yount,
Eddie Miller and Dub Williams

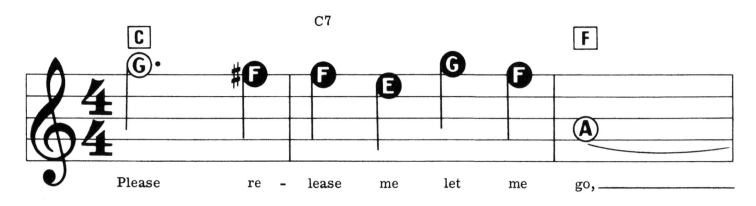

Please   re - lease   me   let   me   go, _____

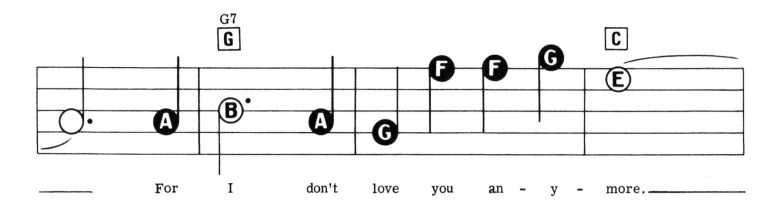

_____   For   I   don't   love   you   an - y - more. _____

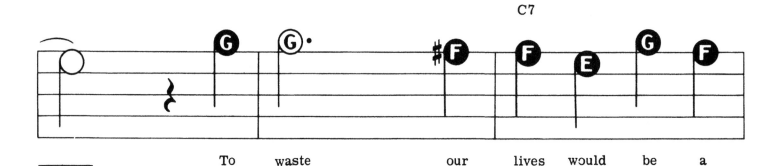

_____   To   waste   our   lives   would   be   a

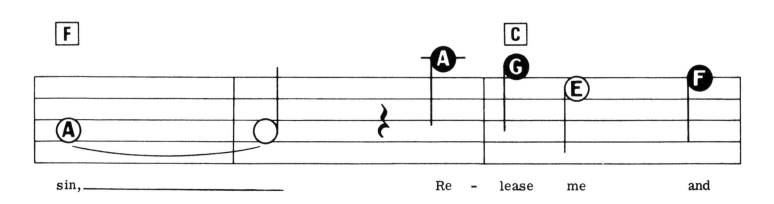

sin, _____   Re - lease   me   and

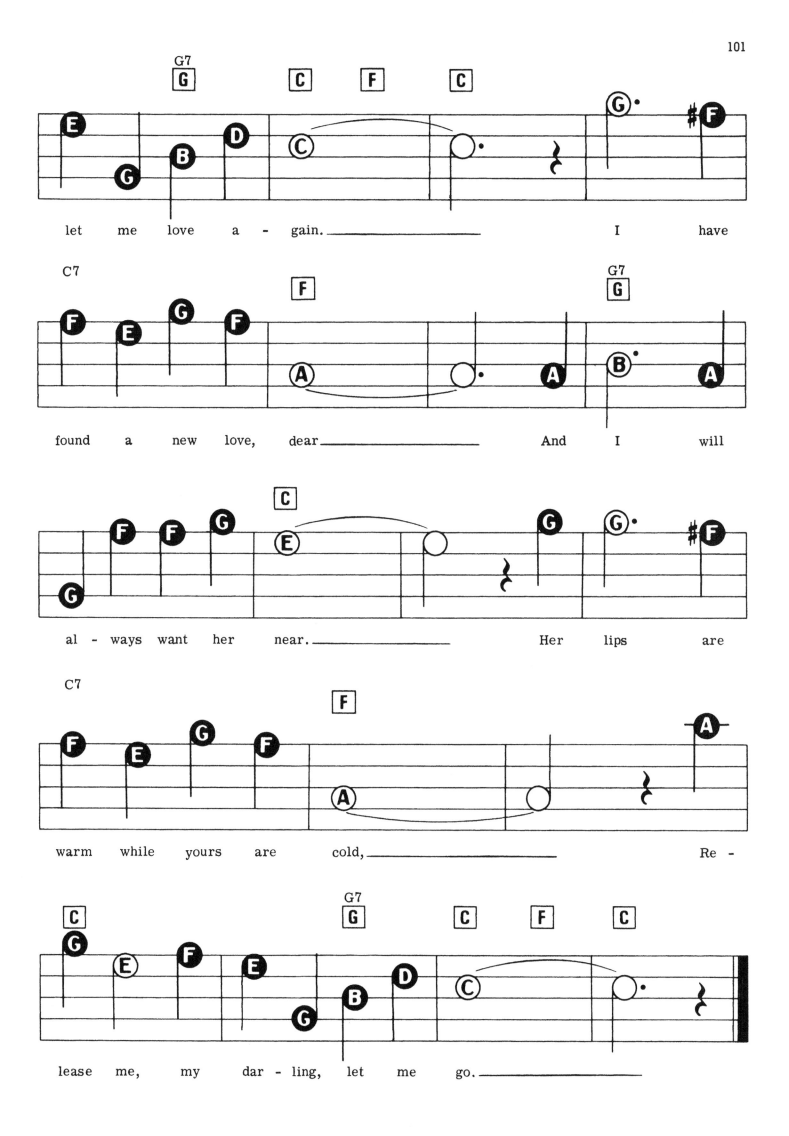

Return to Sender

Registration 4
Rhythm: Rock

Words and Music by Otis Blackwell
and Winfield Scott

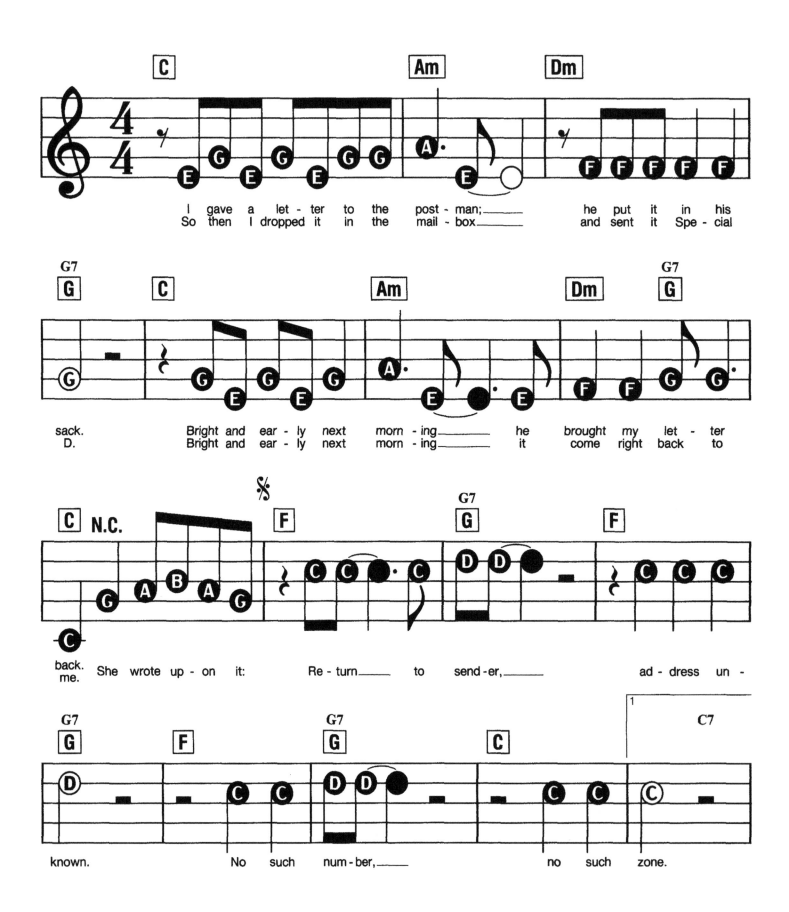

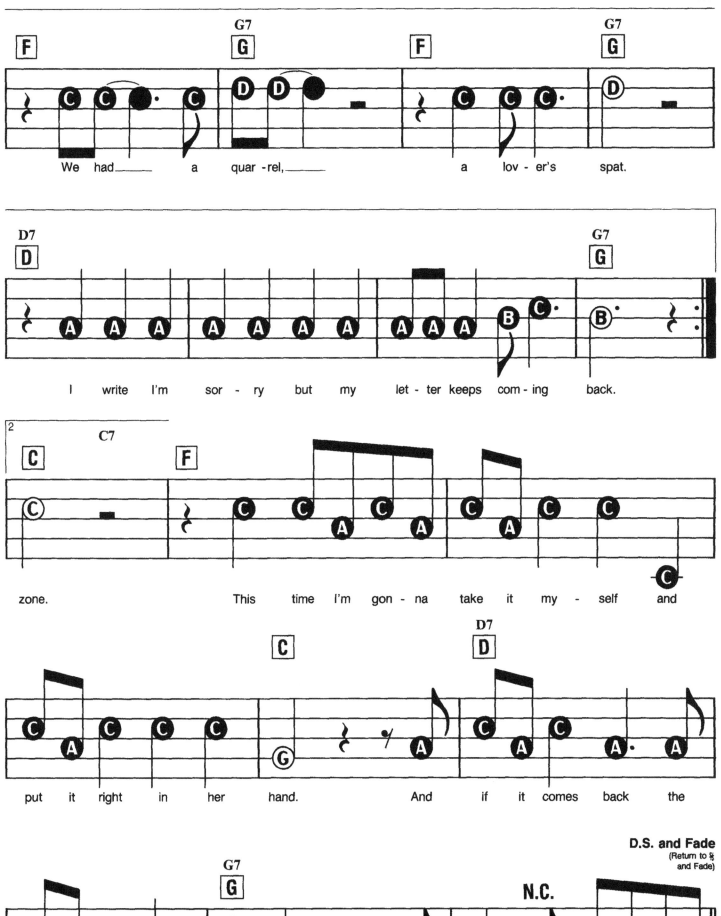

ver - y next day, then I'll un - der - stand_____ the writ - ing on it.

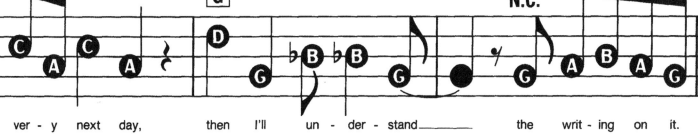

Suspicious Minds

Registration 7
Rhythm: Rock

Words and Music by
Mark James

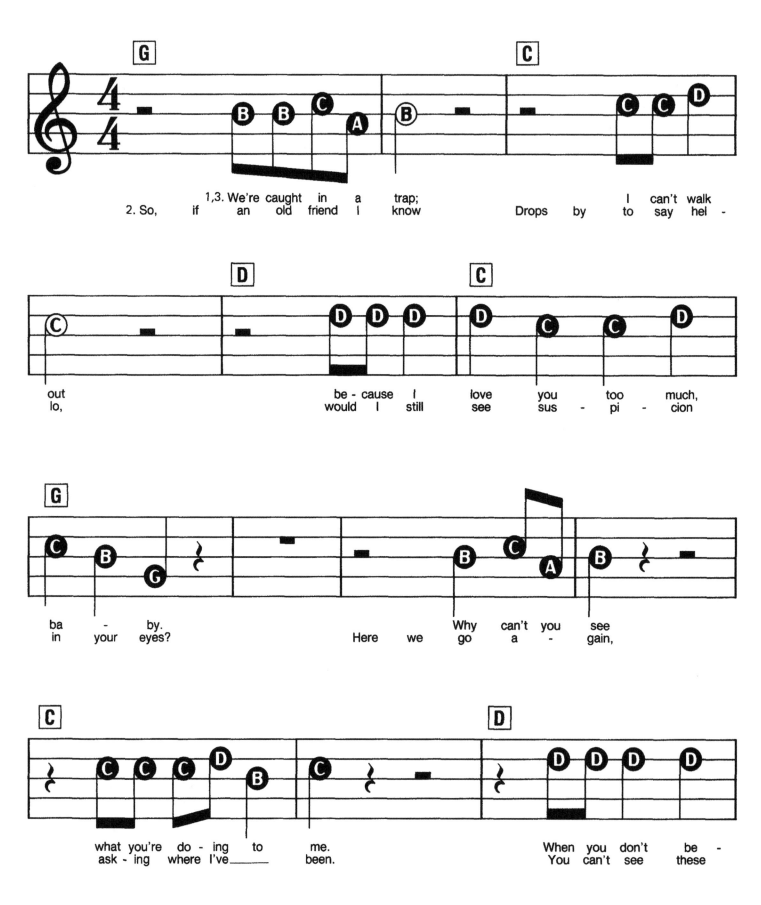

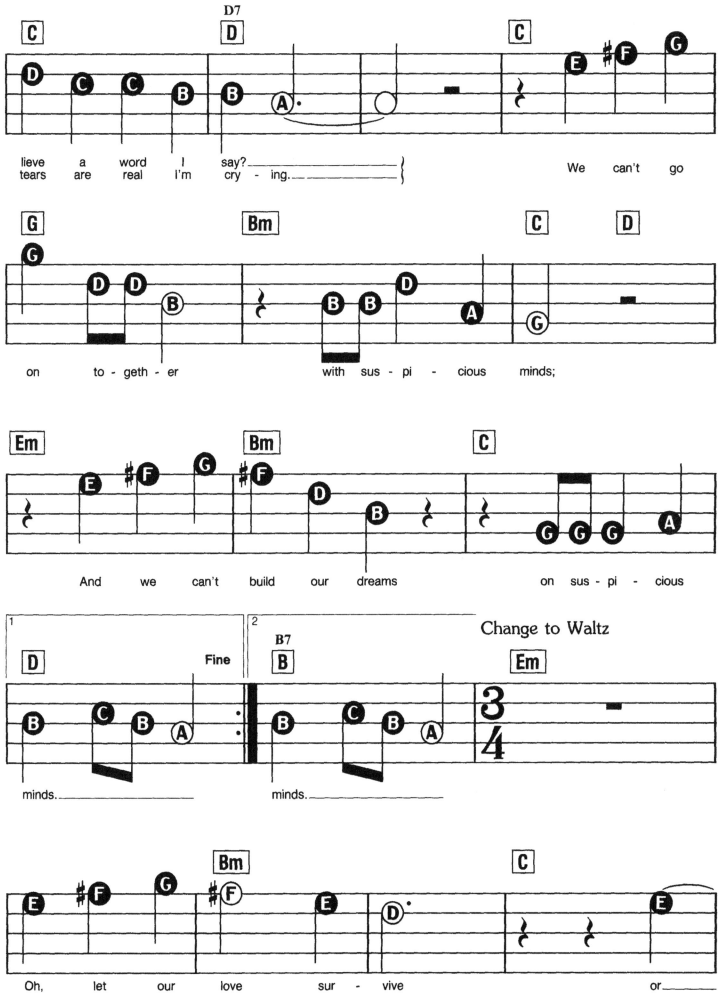

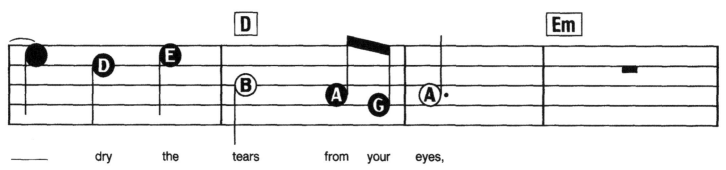

dry the tears from your eyes,

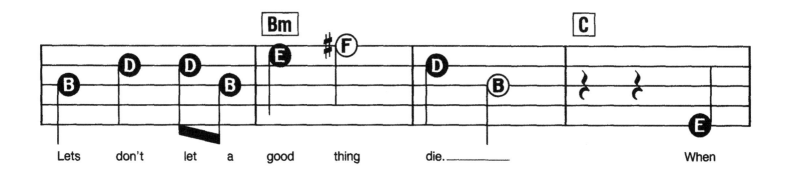

Lets don't let a good thing die.   When

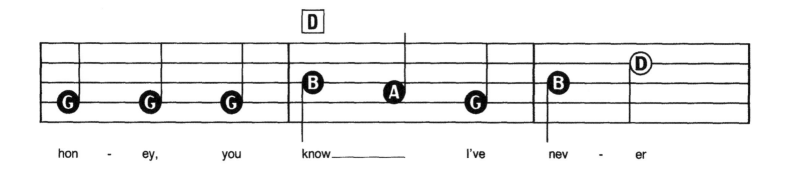

hon - ey, you know   I've nev - er

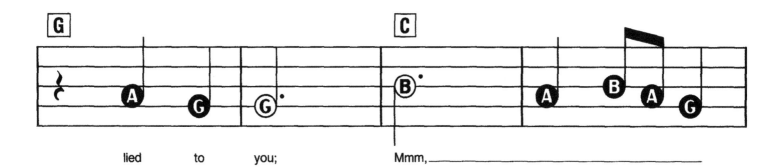

lied to you; Mmm,

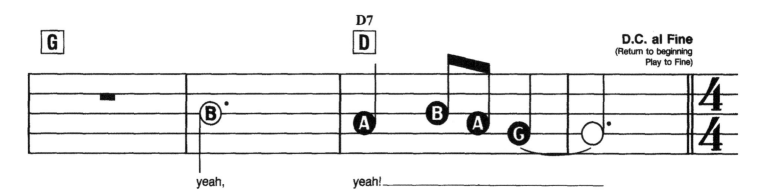

yeah, yeah!

Too Much

Registration 4
Rhythm: Rock

Words and Music by Lee Rosenberg
and Bernard Weiman

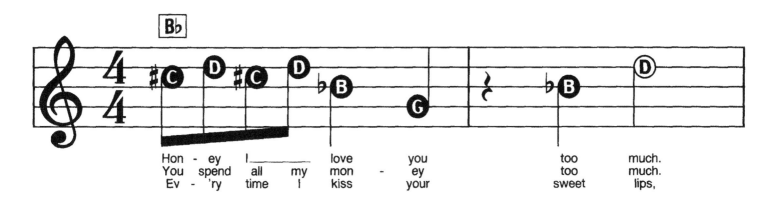

Hon - ey I ___ love you too much.
You spend all my mon - ey too much.
Ev - 'ry time I kiss your sweet lips,

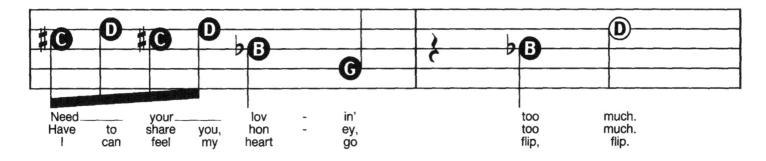

Need your lov - in' too much.
Have to share you, hon - ey, too much.
I can feel my heart go flip, flip.

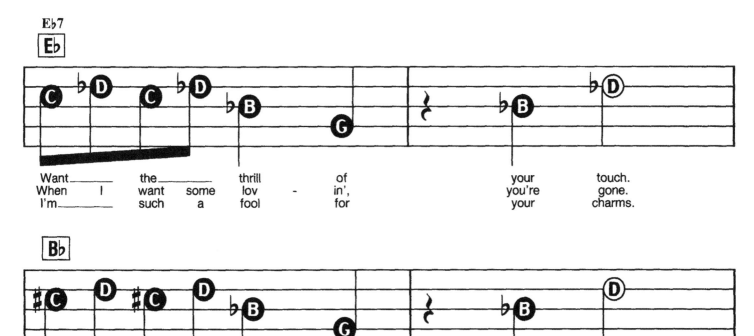

Want the thrill of your touch.
When I want some lov - in', you're gone.
I'm such a fool for your charms.

Gee, I can't hold you too much.
Don't you know you're treat - in' me wrong.
Take me back, my ba - by, in your arms.

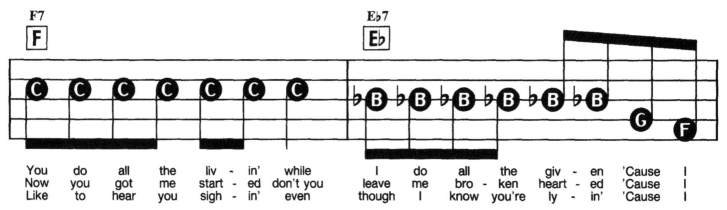

You do all the liv - in' while I do all the giv - en 'Cause I
Now you got me start - ed don't you leave me bro - ken heart - ed 'Cause I
Like to hear you sigh - in' even though I know you're ly - in' 'Cause I

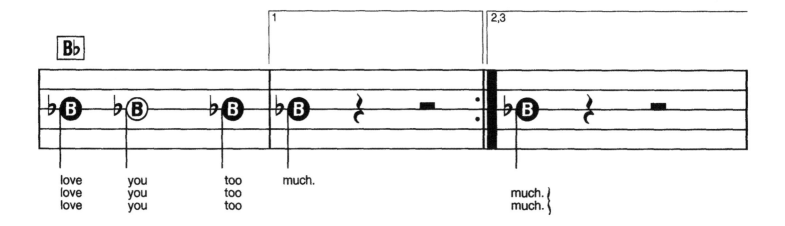

love you too much.
love you too
love you too much.

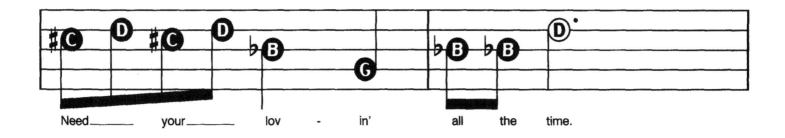

Need_____ your_____ lov - in' all the time.

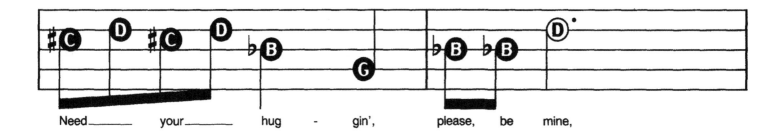

Need_____ your_____ hug - gin', please, be mine,

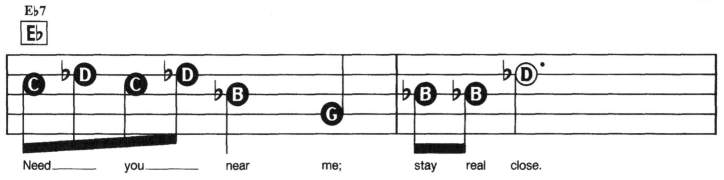

Eb7

Eb

Need_____ you_____ near me; stay real close.

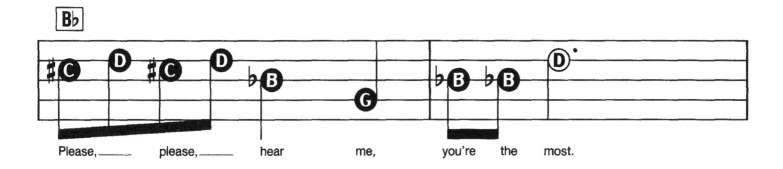

Bb

Please,_____ please,_____ hear me, you're the most.

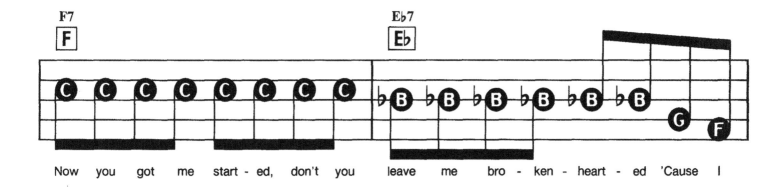

F7

F

Now you got me start-ed, don't you leave me bro-ken-heart-ed 'Cause I

Eb7

Eb

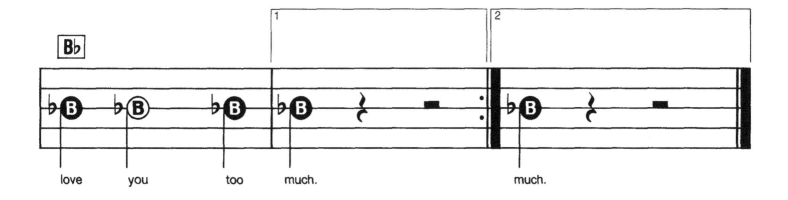

Bb

love you too much.

much.

(Let Me Be Your)
Teddy Bear

Registration 1
Rhythm: Rock

Words and Music by Kal Mann
and Bernie Lowe

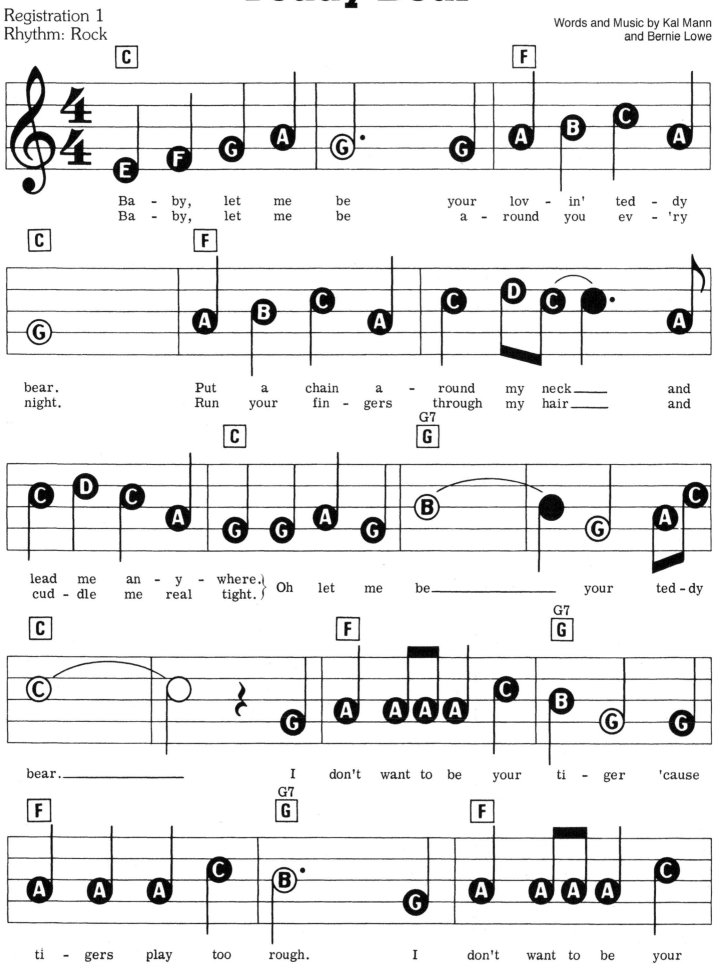

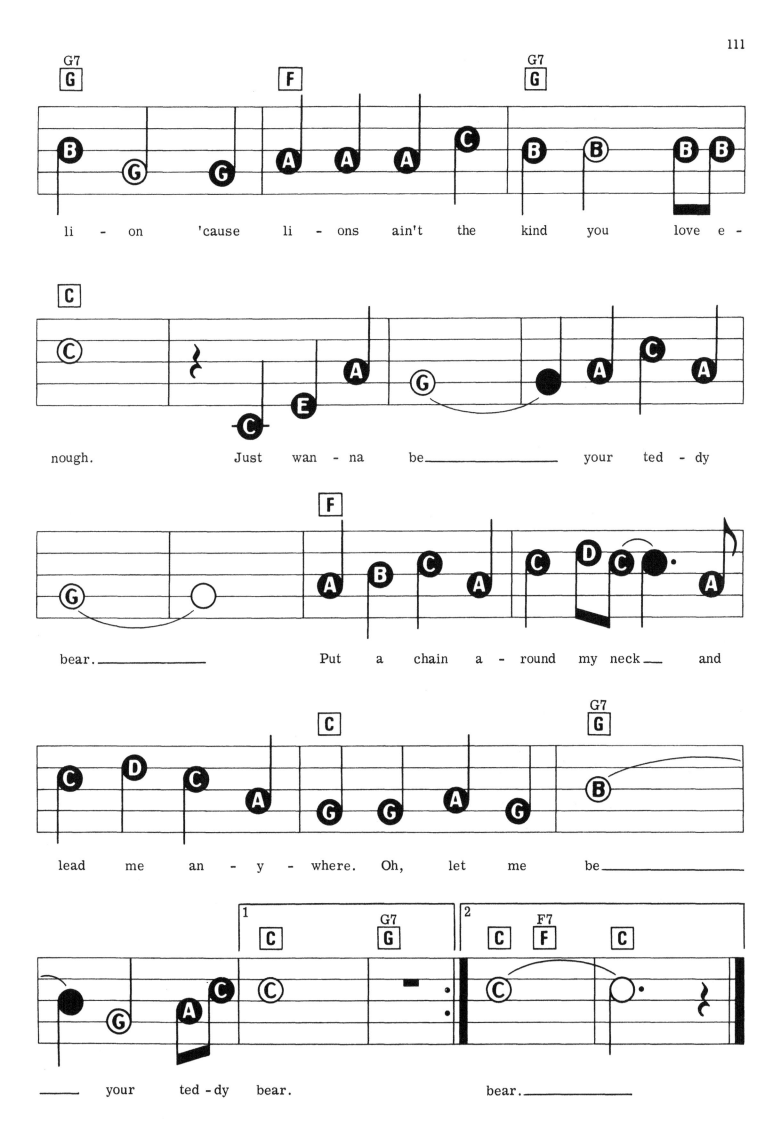

That's All Right

Registration 4
Rhythm: Rock

Words and Music by
Arthur Crudup

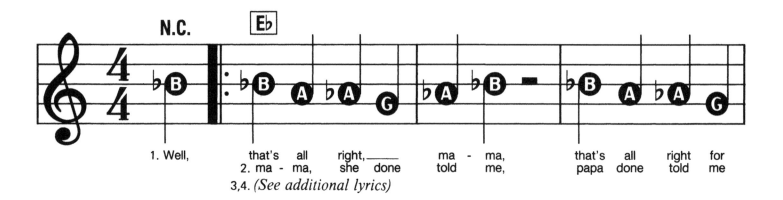

1. Well, that's all right,_____ ma - ma, that's all right for
2. ma - ma, she done told me, papa done told me
3,4. *(See additional lyrics)*

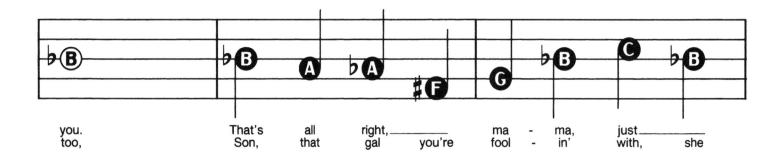

you.
too,

That's all right,_____ ma - ma, just_____
Son, that gal you're fool - in' with, she

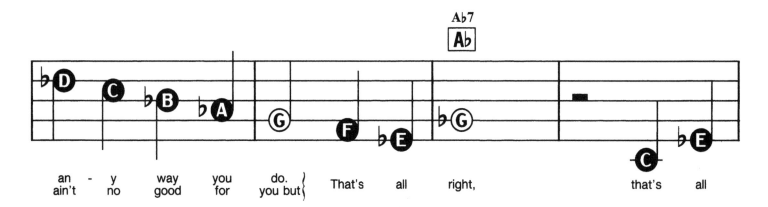

an - y way you do.
ain't no good for you but

That's all right, that's all

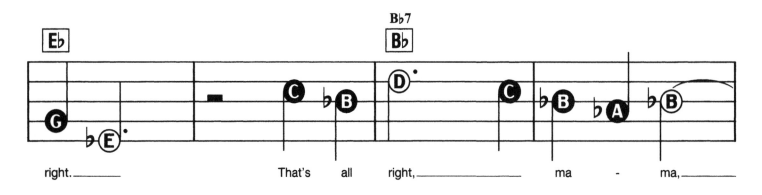

right._____

That's all right,_____ ma - ma,_____

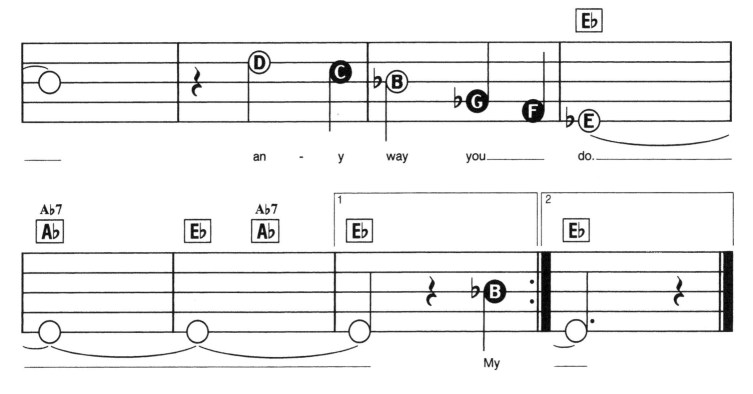

an - y way you___ do.___

My

Additional Lyrics

3. I'm leavin' town tomorrow, leavin' town for sure,
Then you won't be bothered with me hangin' 'round your door,
But that's all right, that's all right.
That's all right, mama, any way you do.

4. I oughta mind my papa, guess I'm not too smart.
If I was I'd leave you, go before you break my heart,
But that's all right, that's all right.
That's all right, mama, any way you do.

Treat Me Nice

Registration 9
Rhythm: Rock

Words and Music by Jerry Leiber
and Mike Stoller

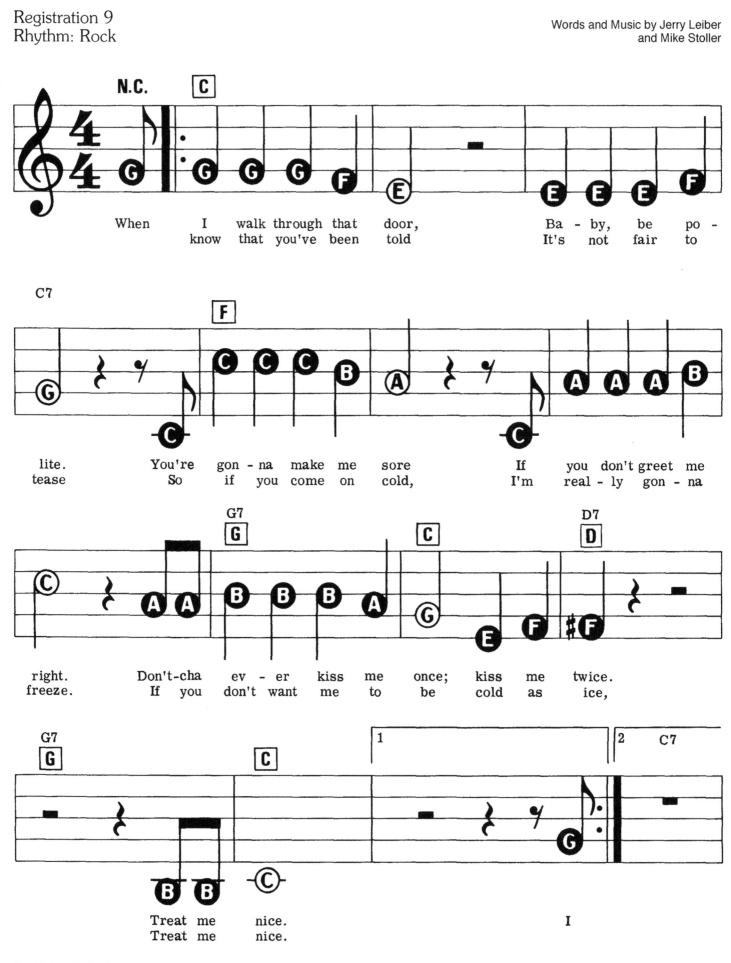

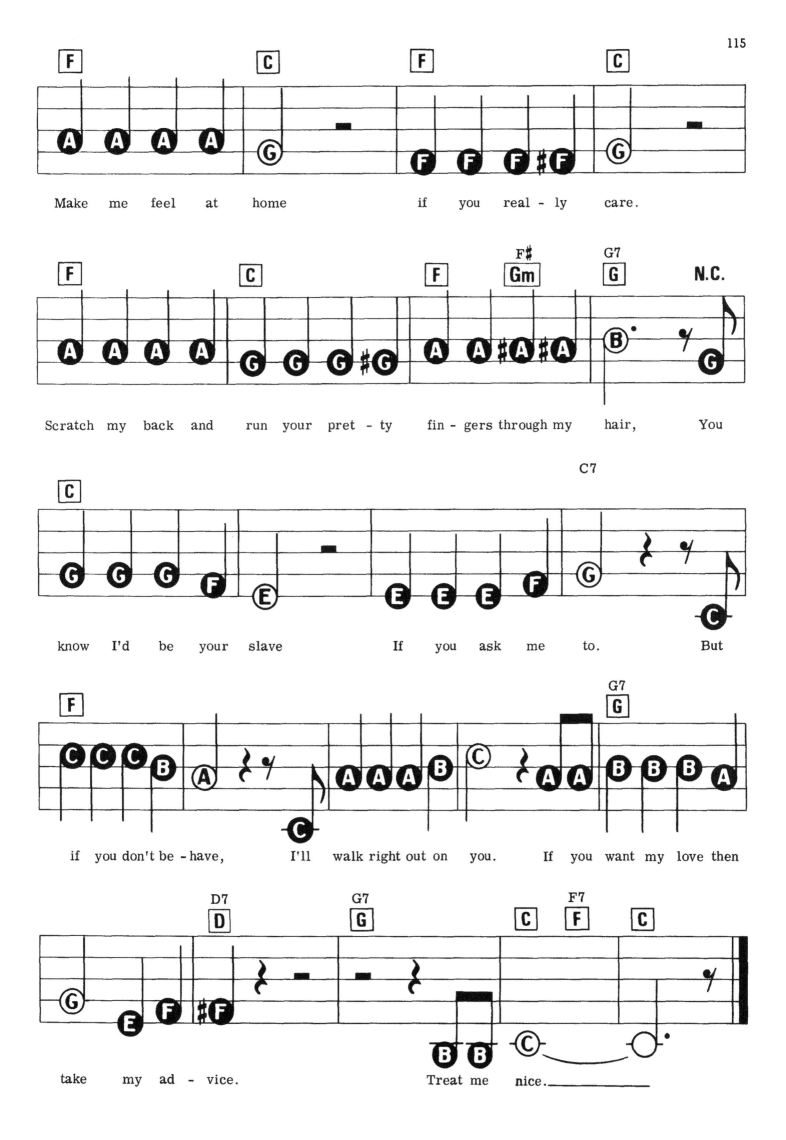

Viva Las Vegas

Registration 5
Rhythm: Rock

Words and Music by Doc Pomus
and Mort Shuman

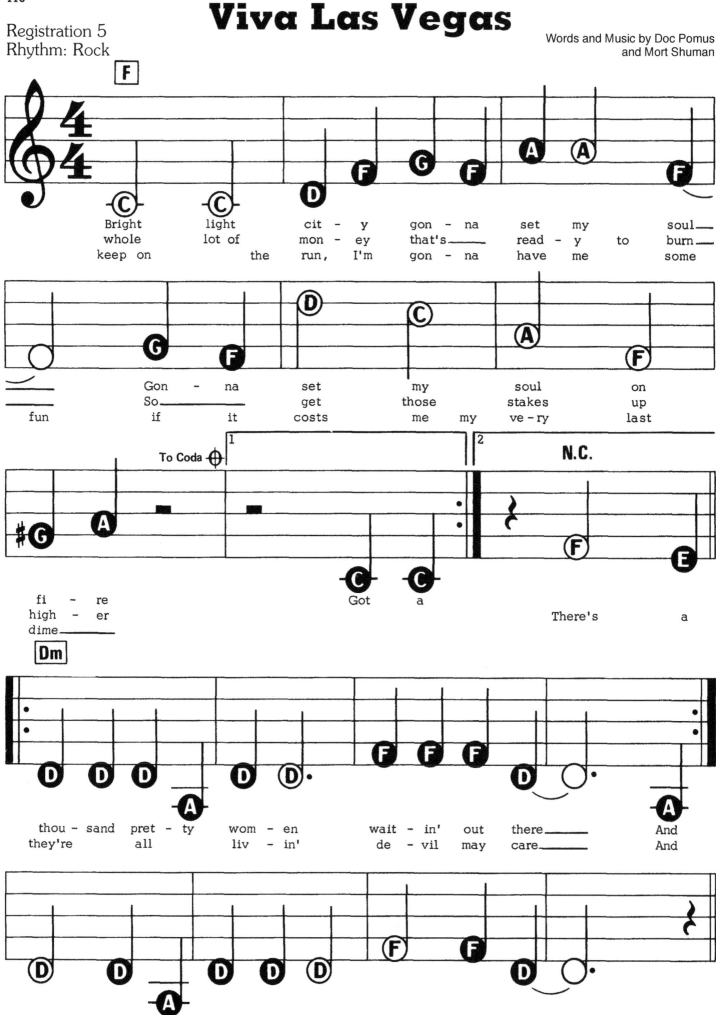

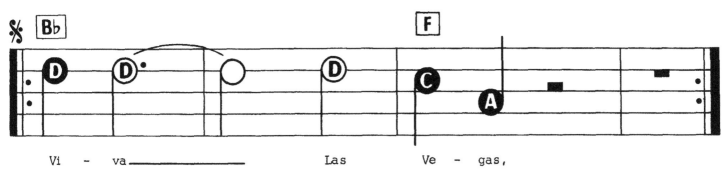

Vi - va_____ Las Ve - gas,

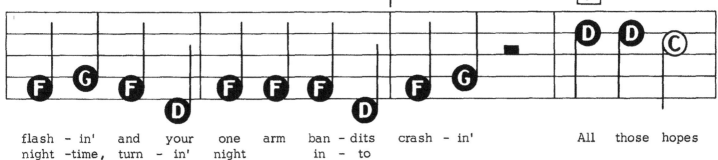

Vi - va Las Ve - gas with your ne - on
Vi - va Las Ve - gas turn - in' day in - to

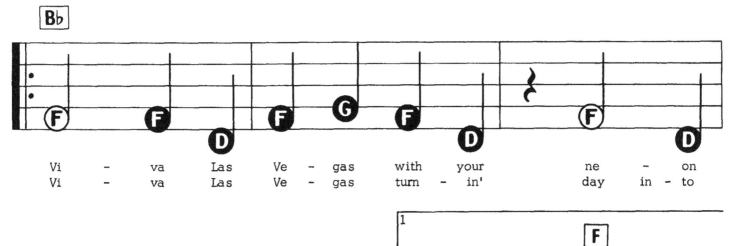

flash - in' and your one arm ban - dits crash - in' All those hopes
night -time, turn - in' night in - to

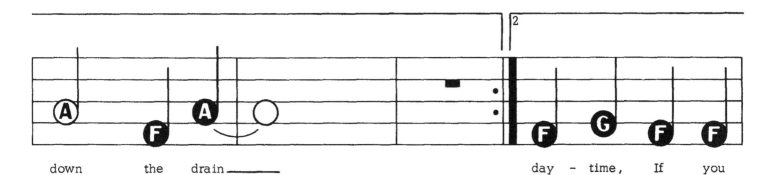

down the drain_____ day - time, If you

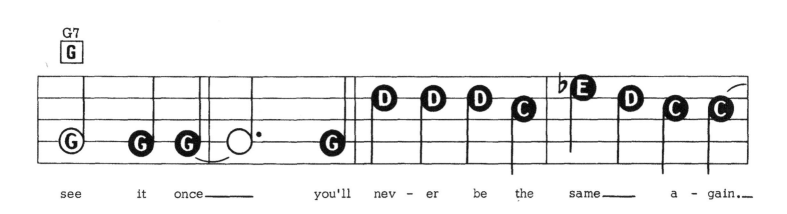

see it once_____ you'll nev - er be the same_____ a - gain._____

118

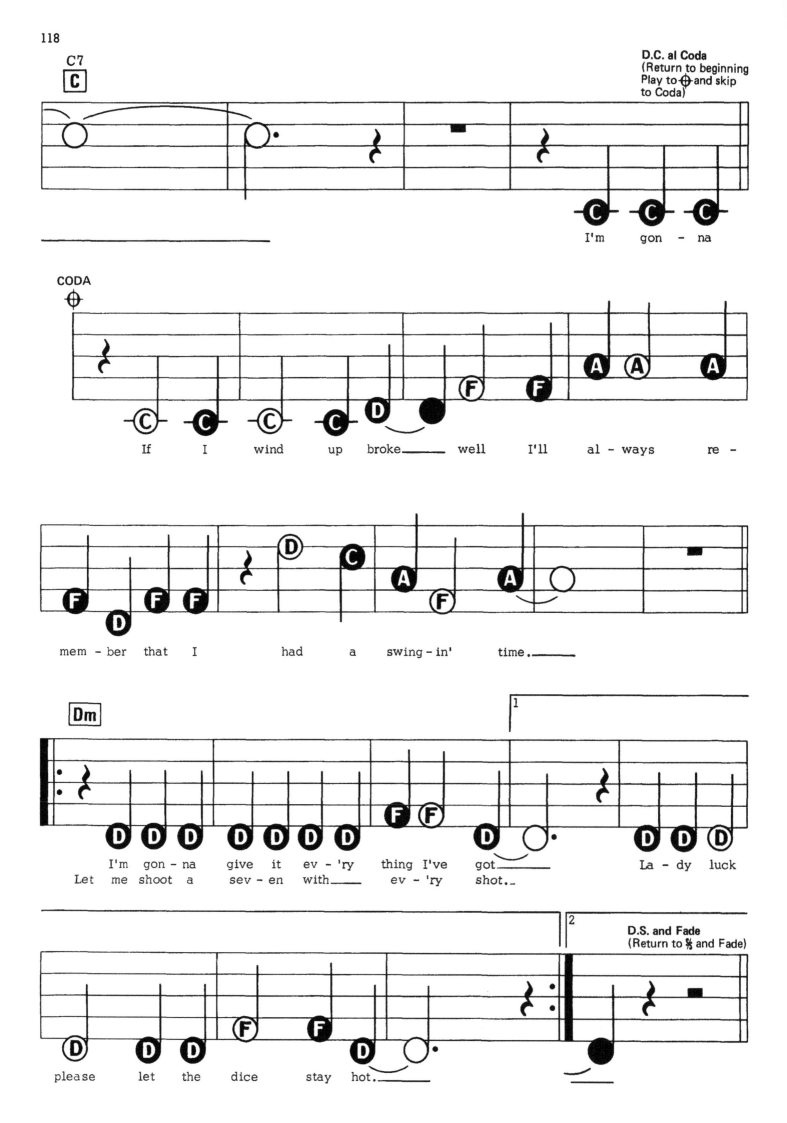

Wear My Ring Around Your Neck

Registration 5
Rhythm: Rock

Words and Music by Bert Carroll
and Russell Moody

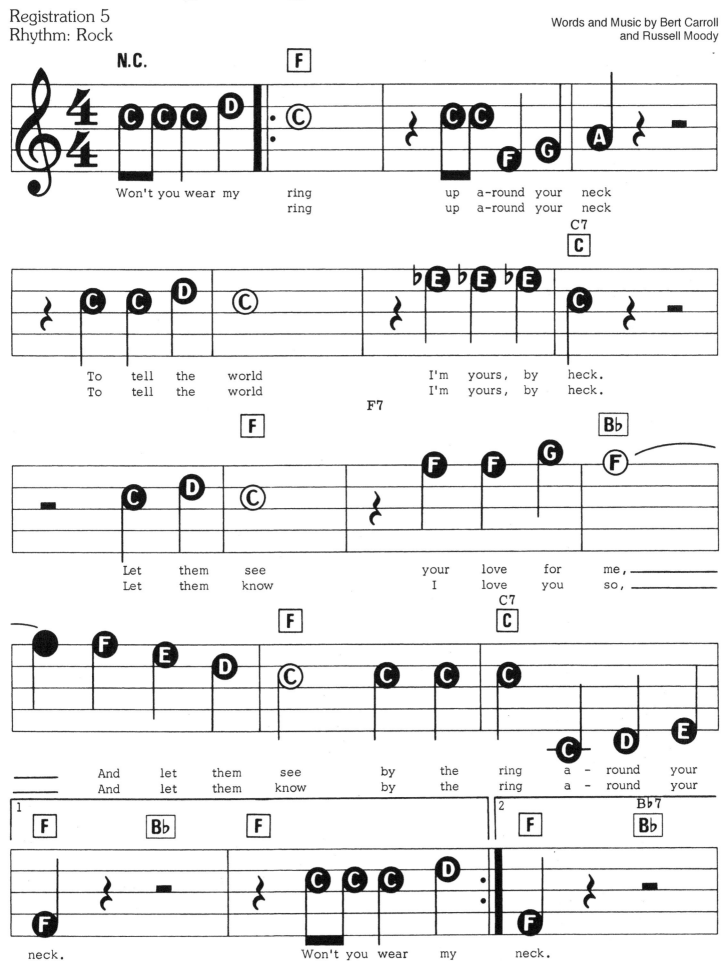

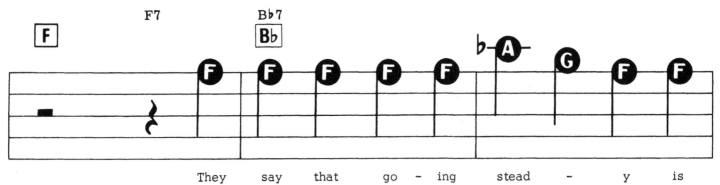

They say that go - ing stead - y is

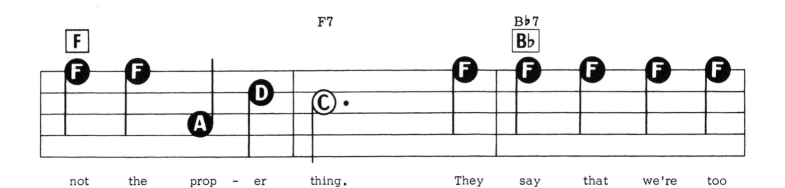

not the prop - er thing. They say that we're too

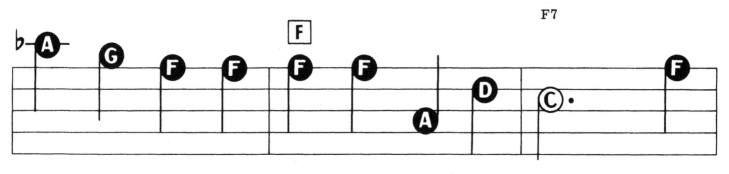

young to know the mean - ing of a ring. I

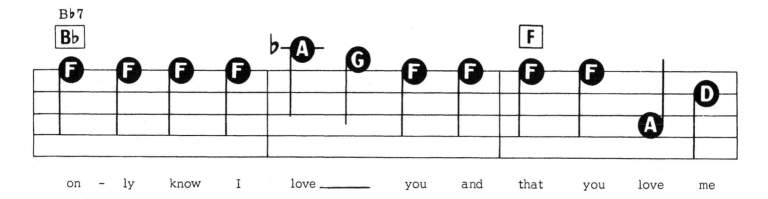

on - ly know I love _____ you and that you love me

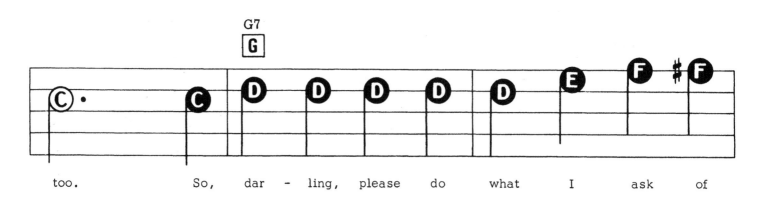

too. So, dar - ling, please do what I ask of

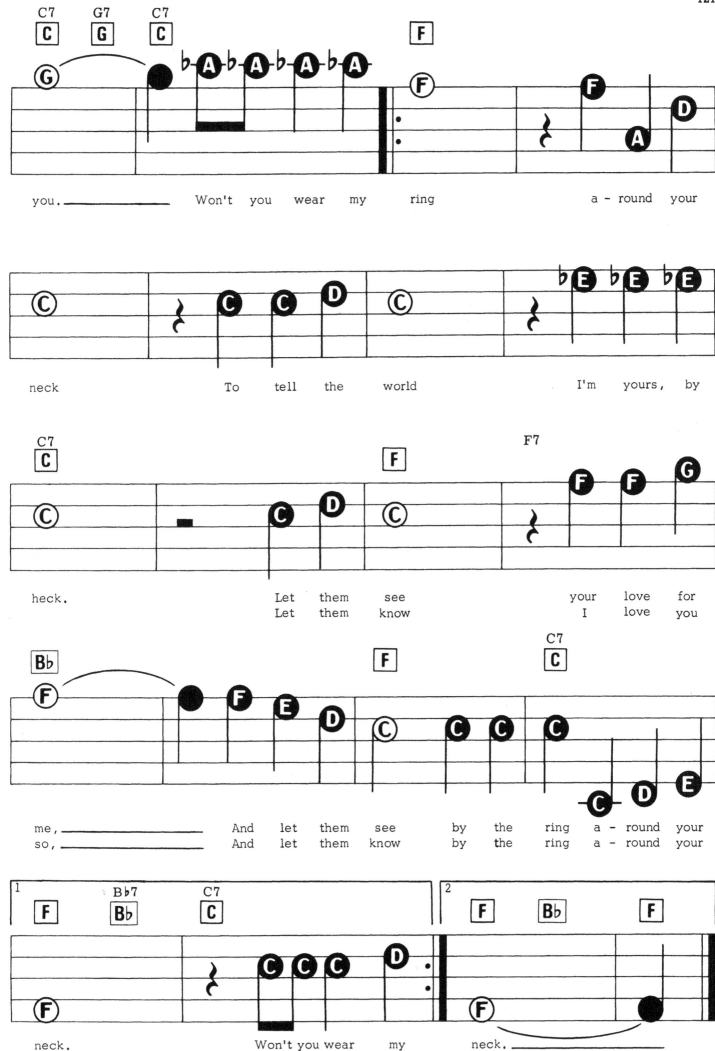

The Wonder of You

Registration 4
Rhythm: Rock

Words and Music by
Baker Knight

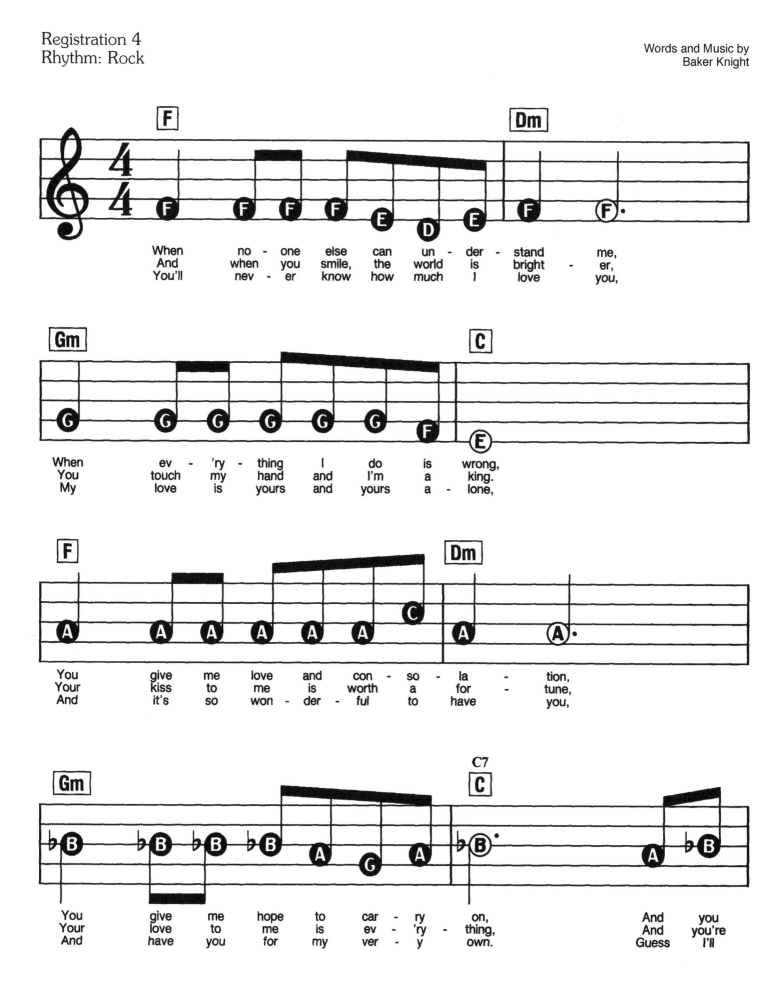

When no - one else can un - der - stand me,
And when you smile, the world is bright - er,
You'll nev - er know how much I love you,

When ev - 'ry - thing I do is wrong,
You touch my hand and I'm a king.
My love is yours and yours a - lone,

You give me love and con - so - la - tion,
Your kiss to me is worth a for - tune,
And it's so won - der - ful to have you,

You give me hope to car - ry on,
Your love to me is ev - 'ry - thing,
And have you for my ver - y own.

And you
And you're
Guess I'll

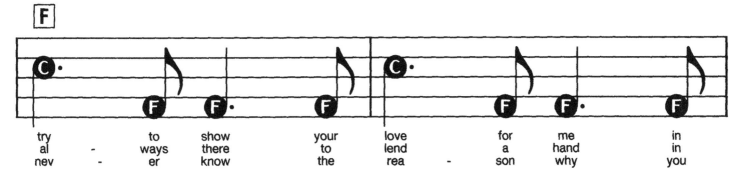

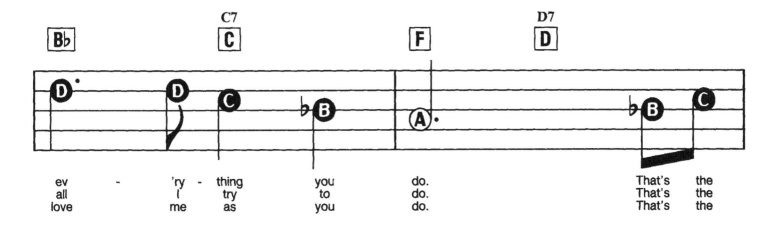

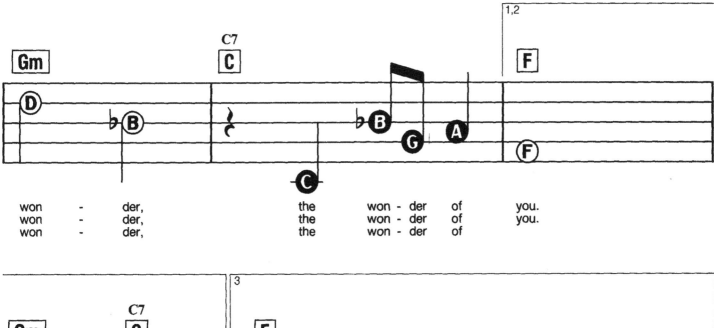

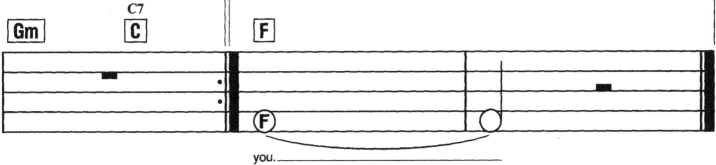

Wooden Heart

Registration 4
Rhythm: Slow Rock

Words and Music by Fred Wise,
Ben Weisman, Kay Twomey
and Berthold Kaempfert

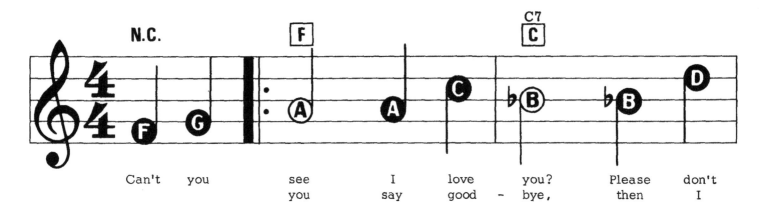

Can't you see I love you? Please don't
you say good - bye, then I

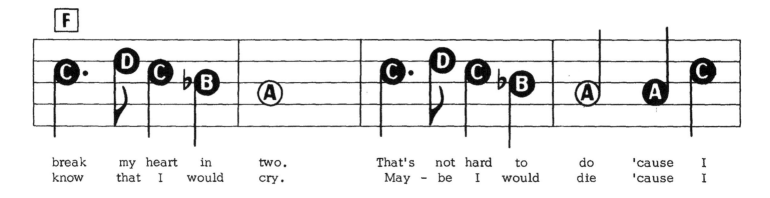

break my heart in two. That's not hard to do 'cause I
know that I would cry. May - be I would die 'cause I

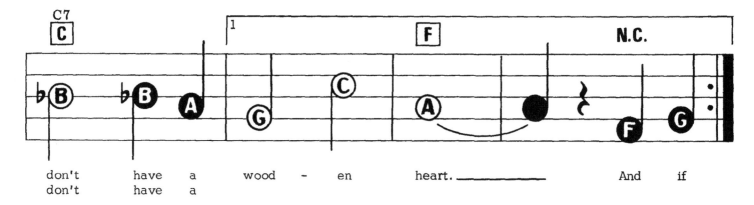

don't have a wood - en heart. ____ And if
don't have a

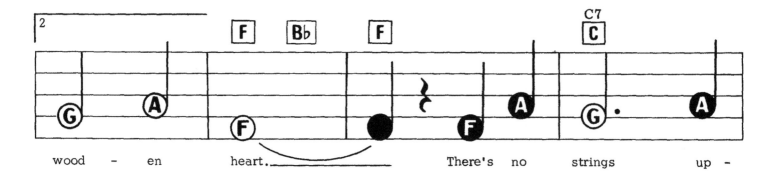

wood - en heart. ____ There's no strings up -

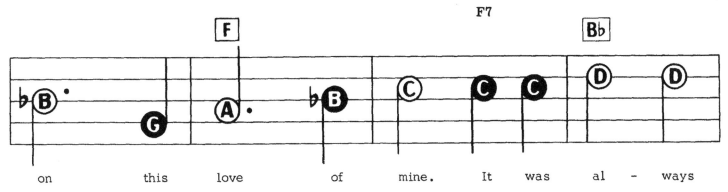

on this love of mine. It was al - ways

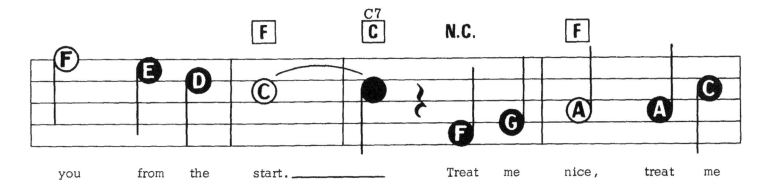

you from the start._____ Treat me nice, treat me

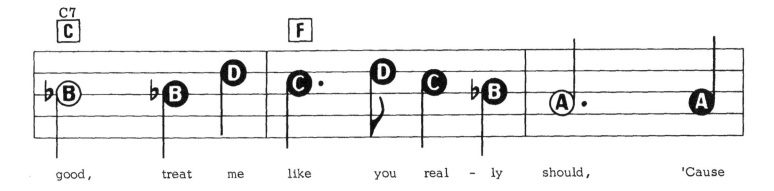

good, treat me like you real - ly should, 'Cause

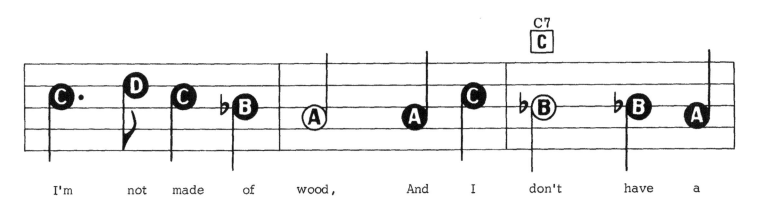

I'm not made of wood, And I don't have a

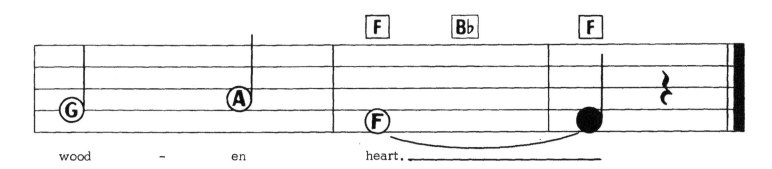

wood - en heart._____

You Don't Know Me
from CLAMBAKE

Registration 5
Rhythm: Slow Rock or Rock

Words and Music by Cindy Walker
and Eddy Arnold

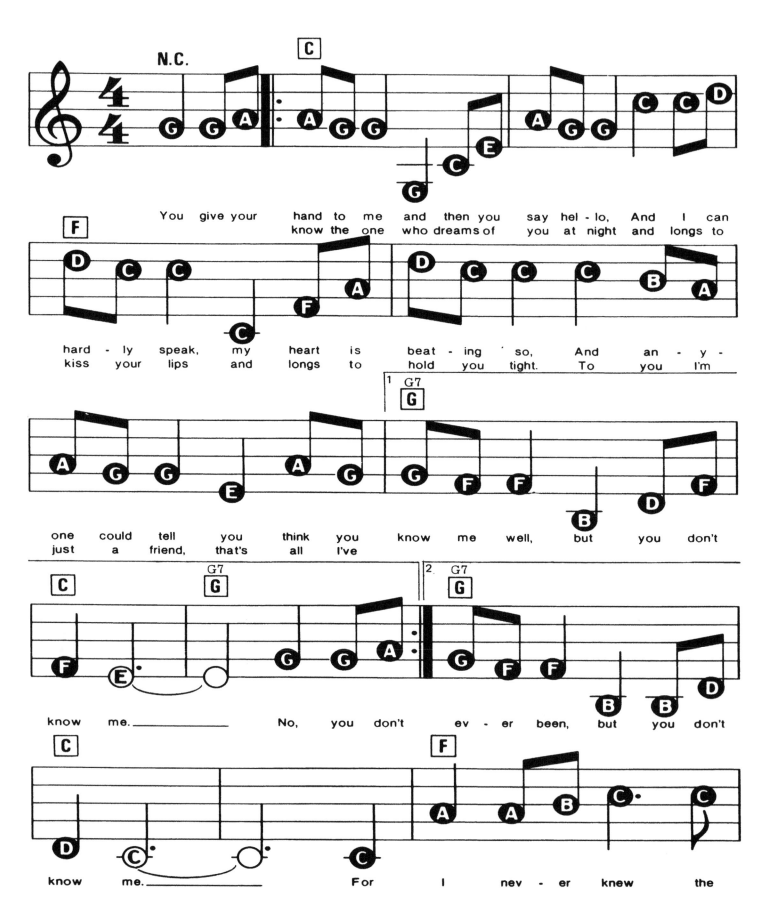

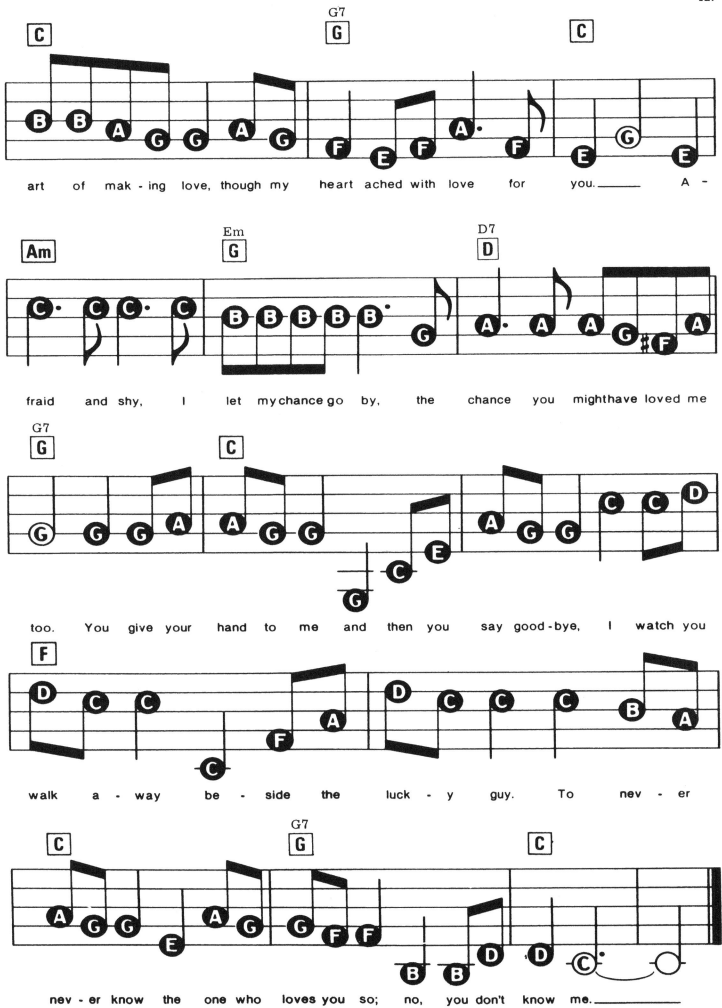

Registration Guide

- Match the Registration number on the song to the corresponding numbered category below. Select and activate an instrumental sound available on your instrument.

- Choose an automatic rhythm appropriate to the mood and style of the song. (Consult your Owner's Guide for proper operation of automatic rhythm features.)

- Adjust the tempo and volume controls to comfortable settings.

Registration

1	Mellow	Flutes, Clarinet, Oboe, Flugel Horn, Trombone, French Horn, Organ Flutes
2	Ensemble	Brass Section, Sax Section, Wind Ensemble, Full Organ, Theater Organ
3	Strings	Violin, Viola, Cello, Fiddle, String Ensemble, Pizzicato, Organ Strings
4	Guitars	Acoustic/Electric Guitars, Banjo, Mandolin, Dulcimer, Ukulele, Hawaiian Guitar
5	Mallets	Vibraphone, Marimba, Xylophone, Steel Drums, Bells, Celesta, Chimes
6	Liturgical	Pipe Organ, Hand Bells, Vocal Ensemble, Choir, Organ Flutes
7	Bright	Saxophones, Trumpet, Mute Trumpet, Synth Leads, Jazz/Gospel Organs
8	Piano	Piano, Electric Piano, Honky Tonk Piano, Harpsichord, Clavi
9	Novelty	Melodic Percussion, Wah Trumpet, Synth, Whistle, Kazoo, Perc. Organ
10	Bellows	Accordion, French Accordion, Mussette, Harmonica, Pump Organ, Bagpipes